RECONSTRUCTION

The Rebuilding of the United States After the Civil War

Judy Dodge Cummings

Illustrated by Micah Rauch

Nomad Press
A division of Nomad Communications
10 9 8 7 6 5 4 3 2 1

This book was manufactured by Versa Press,
East Peoria, Illinois, United States
November 2021, Job #J21-05590

ISBN Softcover: 978-1-61930-976-0
ISBN Hardcover: 978-1-61930-973-9

Educational Consultant, Marla Conn

Questions regarding the ordering of this book should be addressed to
Nomad Press
PO Box 1036, Norwich, VT 05055
www.nomadpress.net

Printed in the United States.

More American history titles

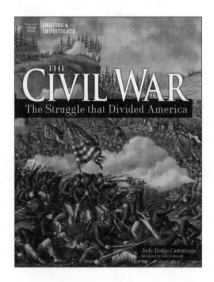

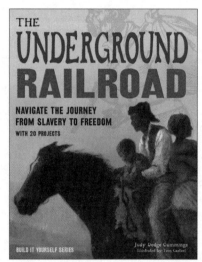

Check out more titles at www.nomadpress.net

Interested
in primary
sources?
PS
**Look for
this icon.**

You can use a smartphone or tablet app to scan the QR codes
and explore more! Cover up neighboring QR codes to make sure you're
scanning the right one. You can find a list of urls on the Resources page.

If the QR code doesn't work, try searching the internet with
the Keyword Prompts to find other helpful sources.

 Reconstruction

Contents

Glossary ▼ Resources ▼ Selected Bibliography ▼ Index

MAP

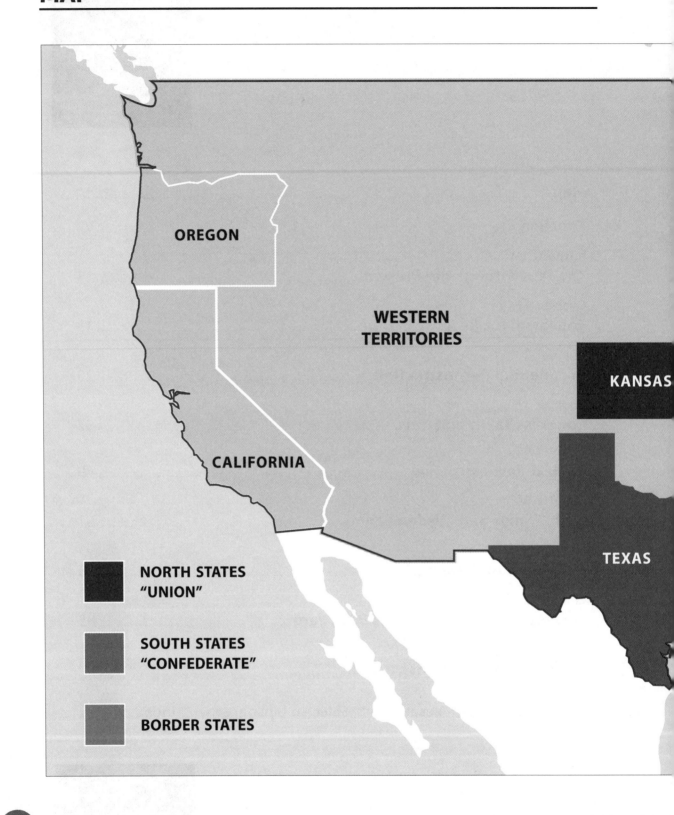

OREGON

WESTERN
TERRITORIES

KANSAS

CALIFORNIA

TEXAS

NORTH STATES
"UNION"

SOUTH STATES
"CONFEDERATE"

BORDER STATES

MAP VII

TIMELINE

April 12, 1861:
The Civil War begins with the Battle of Fort Sumter.

January 1, 1863:
President Abraham Lincoln signs the Emancipation Proclamation.

December 8, 1863:
President Lincoln announces the Proclamation of Amnesty and Reconstruction Act.

March 3, 1865:
The Freedmen's Bureau is created.

April 9, 1865:
The Civil War ends when Confederate General Robert E. Lee surrenders to Union General Ulysses S. Grant.

April 15, 1865:
President Lincoln is assassinated.

May 29, 1865:
President Andrew Johnson announces his Reconstruction plan.

November 1865:
Mississippi becomes the first postwar state to enact a Black Code.

December 6, 1865:
The Thirteenth Amendment is ratified.

December 24, 1865:
The Ku Klux Klan (KKK) is formed.

April 5, 1866:
The Civil Rights Act is passed over President Johnson's veto.

July 16, 1866:
The Freedmen's Bureau is expanded and its powers extended over President Johnson's veto.

July 30, 1866:
The New Orleans Massacre occurs.

1867:
Reconstruction Acts are passed over President Johnson's vetoes.

July 28, 1868:
The Fourteenth Amendment is ratified.

November 3, 1868:
Ulysses S. Grant is elected president.

February 25, 1870:
Hiram Revels is seated in the U.S. Senate as the first Black senator.

February 3, 1870:
The Fifteenth Amendment is ratified.

December 12, 1870:
Joseph H. Rainey is the first Black man elected to the U.S. House of Representatives.

April 20, 1871:
The Ku Klux Klan Act is passed.

June 28, 1872:
The Freedmen's Bureau is abolished.

March 1, 1875:
Another Civil Rights Act is passed outlawing segregation in most public places and in transportation.

March 4, 1877:
Rutherford B. Hayes is inaugurated president.

1877:
Federal troops remain in the South but have no authority to intervene in state decisions, effectively reducing the federal government's power in the South.

Introduction ▶

The Past Informs the Present

What can we learn about the period of time called Reconstruction that will help today?

The period of Reconstruction after the Civil War has much in common with today's world, including a collective wish to see more social, political, and economic equality. We also share many of the same challenges. By paying attention to history, people of the present have a better chance of affecting positive change.

A divided public. Lawmakers with competing visions for the future. Bold newspaper headlines about voting rights, citizenship, and domestic terrorism. While this may sound like the United States of today, these sentences describe the country between 1865 and 1877, during the era called Reconstruction. Similar to the present, Reconstruction was a time of division and turmoil, when Americans struggled to define freedom and determine who should get it.

Reconstruction was a turning point in American history. During the Civil War, from 1861 to 1865, the North and South had fought about two central questions. Should the United States remain one nation? Should enslaved people be freed?

The North won the war. As a result, the 11 Confederate states of the South had to return to the Union on terms set by the North, while the 4 million enslaved people in the South were freed.

These two momentous changes raised critical questions that would shape the country's future.

- Should the Southern states be welcomed back with open arms or should they be punished?

- Should former slaves enjoy the same rights and freedoms as American citizens?

- Should the federal government compensate former slaveholders for the "property" they had to free?

- Should the freed people be compensated for years of stolen labor?

This book tells the story of how nineteenth-century Americans tried to answer these questions. As African Americans gained new political, economic, and social freedoms, the moment felt ripe with the promise of true equality. However, the more Black people asserted their new powers, the more Southern whites resisted. By 1877, the reforming spirit of Reconstruction was gone, and white supremacists regained control in the South.

RECONSTRUCT

From 2008 to 2018, the United States spent at least $40 million to maintain Confederate statues, museums, cemeteries, homes, and libraries. Very few of these sites mention the lives of enslaved people.

WHOSE HERITAGE MATTERS

Although Confederates lost the Civil War 150 years ago, more than 1,700 Confederate markers dot the United States landscape from Florida to Washington State. From 1924 to 2021, a statue of Confederate General Robert E. Lee (1807–1870) sat astride a horse in Emancipation Park in Charlottesville, Virginia. When City Councilor Kristin Szakos suggested in 2012 that perhaps it was time to remove the statue from the park, people gasped.

White supremacists clash with police in Charlottesville, Virginia, 2017.

Credit: Evan Nesterak (CC BY 2.0)

View the map of Confederate markers compiled by the Southern Poverty Law Center at this website.

In what area of the country are most of the Confederate markers located? What explains this?

public symbols Confederacy map

Szakos recalled in a 2013 interview, "I felt like I had put a stick in the ground and kind of ugly stuff bubbled up from it." The statue of General Lee remained.

However, by 2015, the issue of Confederate symbols in public places was being debated in communities across the South. People who wanted monuments and memorials removed and streets and schools renamed said the Confederacy represented white supremacy and had no place in modern America.

Opponents of removal denied these markers were racist. They insisted the markers symbolized Southern heritage and should not be erased.

In 2016, Charlottesville high school student Zyahna Bryant petitioned the city council to remove the Lee statue from the city center. "It makes us feel uncomfortable," she wrote, "and it is very offensive." The council voted to take down the statute, but opponents immediately sued and a judge issued an injunction blocking its removal. Charlottesville became a powder keg waiting for a spark.

That explosion was ignited the morning of August 12, 2017. White supremacists dressed in combat gear and wielding Confederate flags rallied in Charlottesville to support keeping Lee's statue in the park. They were met by hundreds of counter-protesters. At first, the two sides traded only verbal insults, but soon they were throwing punches. Virginia's governor declared a state of emergency and the police and National Guard cleared the park.

That afternoon, as throngs of counter-protesters marched peacefully toward the downtown, a car plowed into them from behind. The vehicle was driven by 20-year-old James Alex Fields, a white supremacist with a history of mental instability. Pedestrians screamed as bodies flew into the air. "It was probably the scariest thing I've ever seen in my life," said Robert Armengol, a student at the University of Virginia. One woman was killed and 34 people were injured.

The violence in Charlottesville was just one event in a series of dramatic confrontations over the fate of the hundreds of Confederate markers scattered throughout the United States.

The nation's inability to agree on what these symbols represent is just one reason why Americans need to better understand Reconstruction.

REACTION TO A MASSACRE

It took a massacre for Southern communities to begin removing Confederate flags and markers from public places. In 2015, Dylann Roof killed nine Black people at the Emanuel African Methodist Episcopal Church, a historic Black church in Charleston, South Carolina. Following the murders, investigators discovered a website of Roof's that contained dozens of pictures of him visiting Confederate heritage sites and posing with the Confederate flag. News of his white supremacist views led to a nation-wide movement to remove public commemorations of the Confederacy. State laws protect many of these markers. According to the Southern Poverty Law Center, since the Charleston church shooting, 312 Confederate symbols have been removed or relocated from public spaces. However, more than 2,100 such symbols still remain.

WHAT WAS RECONSTRUCTION?

The most important role in Reconstruction was played by emancipated slaves, known as freedmen and freedwomen, and their Black and white allies. Before the guns of the Civil War had even fallen silent, former slaves were carving out new lives. They adopted new last names, mounted searches for family members who'd been sold off, staked claims to land, and learned to read and write.

Northern Blacks and whites moved south to teach in freedmen schools. They help organize Southern Blacks politically and socially.

RECONSTRUCT

Political power was the central struggle of Reconstruction. The story of this era cannot be told without Republican and Democratic lawmakers, both white people and Black. This was a period of high political drama—assassination, impeachment, and the rise of the Radical Republicans.

A scene from the Freedmen's Union Industrial School in Richmond, Virginia

Many parts of the South, including Atlanta, Georgia, were left in ruins after the Civil War.

At Reconstruction's peak, Congress passed three constitutional amendments that abolished slavery, established the principal of equality for all persons, and prohibited racial discrimination in voting. For the first time in history, Black men went to the polls by the thousands to cast their vote, electing almost 2,000 former slaves and free Black people to federal, state, and local government. The Republican party worked to achieve an interracial democracy built on the ashes of slavery, while Democrats watched their power—built on the foundation of white supremacy—ebb.

However, Reconstruction is an inspiring story with a tragic ending. By the late 1860s, white supremacist groups had unleashed a brutal campaign of terror throughout the South. When an economic depression struck in 1873, the Republican Party grew more concerned with economic stability than racial equality.

> To help navigate the present, Americans must understand their past.

Reconstruction's death knell was sounded when the U.S. Supreme Court issued a series of decisions that dismantled legal protections for African Americans. By the end of the 1890s, the Democratic Party had regained power in the South and constructed a system of racial segregation that lasted for decades.

WHY DOES IT MATTER?

The Reconstruction era offers both hope and caution for modern America. The hope lies in the fact that for the brief window from 1865 to 1877, democracy expanded because Americans worked across racial lines to bring about positive change.

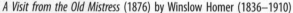

A Visit from the Old Mistress (1876) by Winslow Homer (1836–1910)

The constitutional amendments passed during Reconstruction were not enforced, but they did not disappear. When the Civil Rights Movement expanded in the 1950s, activists based their fight for racial equality on the constitutional changes their forefathers and mothers had fought for a century earlier.

Reconstruction is also a cautionary tale. White supremacy, violence, and indifference killed Reconstruction—problems on the rise again in the early twenty-first century. According to the Southern Poverty Law Center, between 2015 and 2019, the number of hate groups in the United States increased 30 percent. According to an October 2020 survey, 61 percent of Americans believe the United States could be on the verge of another civil war.

> **America is once again deeply divided, and political conversations tend to be damaging and dysfunctional rather than reasonable and productive.**

Reconstruction was a pivotal period in American history, when the nation tried to remake itself into a more perfect union. The story of Reconstruction in the following chapters proves that if enough reform-minded individuals work together, powerful and positive change can occur. But Reconstruction also illustrates how fragile democracy is, a vital lesson for twenty-first-century Americans.

KEY QUESTIONS

- Why is it important to study history, including the controversial issues and events of the past?
- Why do people disagree about removing Confederate statues? What is your opinion about the statues?

LAST RIDE

In April 2019, Virginia State Judge Richard Moore ruled in favor of maintaining the statue of General Robert E. Lee. Moore stated that Lee's statue in Charlottesville was a war memorial not a tribute to racism. Thus, it is protected by a 1997 state law that prohibits removing or altering such markers. However, in April 2021, the Virginia Supreme Court ruled that war memorials erected before the 1997 law were not protected. This ruling has cleared the way for the city council to remove Lee's statute. In July 2021, the statue was removed, along with one of Confederate General Stonewall Jackson (1824–1863).

TEXT TO WORLD

Does your school have a mascot? Do you know of any controversy that has erupted over that mascot? Some organizations have changed their mascots to better reflect the values of today. What do you think of this?

THE PAST INFORMS
THE PRESENT

A MONUMENTAL HISTORY

Monuments designed to honor places, events, or people stand in public places across the United States. Some, such as the Lincoln Memorial and the Statue of Liberty, are classic icons. Others, such as the 2,000-pound African Killer Bee located in Hidalgo, Texas, are less than traditional.

Monuments are often controversial. What is honorable to one person may be offensive to another. Also, the meanings of monuments change as the culture around them evolves. What do monuments reveal about the history, culture, and values of your community?

* **Ask adults, such as parents, teachers, and librarians, to help you make a list of all the historical monuments in your community.** Choose one monument to investigate.

* **Develop a list of questions you want answered about this monument.** Consider the following ideas.

  * When, why, and by whom was this monument erected?

  * What was going in U.S. history when the monument was dedicated?

  * Who owns the land on which the monument sits?

  * Who maintains the structure?

  * What do people today think about this monument?

Language evolves with every generation. Some words widely used 150 years ago to describe races and ethnicities are now considered inaccurate, inappropriate, and even offensive. For example, if you read primary sources from the eighteenth and nineteenth centuries, you'll find lots of references to "colored people." But that phrase does nothing to indicate race. The term "Negro" is another one that has fallen out of use as we've accepted it was used by white people to indicate the inferiority of Black people. Other terms are too offensive to even use in this book. Today, the preferred term is "Black people." We also use "African Americans" when referring to Black Americans of African descent. As we learn more, we can do better with our language.

- **Investigate the monument's origins and present use.** The internet is a handy place to start, but you can also interview your local historical society, librarian, or chamber of commerce.

- **Based on the answers to your questions, what does this monument reveal about the historical beliefs and values of your community?** Have those values and beliefs changed over time? What evidence do you have of this change?

- **What is your opinion of this monument?** Should it remain in your community, be removed, or be expanded or altered in some way to reflect deeper historical insights about the era in which it was erected? What might the consequences be for each action?

- **Design a pamphlet that reflects your opinion about the monument.** The purpose of the pamphlet will depend on your opinion. If you think the monument should remain as is, you might design an advertisement to encourage people to visit. If you think the monument should be removed, your pamphlet might be a petition to the city government. Share your pamphlet with peers and see how their opinions compare with yours.

> To investigate more, design and distribute a survey to assess community opinion about the monument. Analyze the results of the survey. Do the majority of people agree with your view of the monument? If not, how could you redesign your pamphlet to reflect popular opinion about the future of this public structure?

Inquire & Investigate

VOCAB LAB

Write down what you think each word means. What root words can you find to help you? What does the context of the word tell you?

amendment, discrimination, emancipate, heritage, racism, Reconstruction, and **white supremacy**

Compare your definitions with those of your friends or classmates. Did you all come up with the same meanings? Turn to the text and glossary if you need help.

PARTY HISTORY

We talk a lot in this book about the Democratic and Republican Parties as they existed during and right after the Civil War. But those parties are very different from the Democratic and Republican Parties we have today. In fact, in some ways, it can feel like the two parties switched many of their ideals. During Reconstruction, it was the Democratic Party that argued for states' rights, strict voting laws, and a smaller role for the federal government— exactly what the Republican Party argues for today. While the Democrats were considered to be more conservative in the nineteenth century, today they are more liberal than the Republicans. In this activity, you'll compare and contrast the positions of the two parties, then and now.

- **Research and learn more about the Democratic and Republican Parties as they were after the Civil War and as they are now.** What did they think was the job of the U.S. government? Who did they believe should make decisions that affected people's everyday lives? Who was more conservative? Who was more liberal?

- **Create a series of four charts comparing the parties.** One chart should focus on the Democrat and Republican Parties as they were during Reconstruction. Another should compare the way the two parties are now. A third should examine the Democratic Party during Reconstruction and the Democratic Party of today. And fourth should compare the Republican Party, then and now.

  - How similar are your four charts? How different are they?

  - What can they tell you about how the parties have changed in the past 150 years or so?

To investigate more, research other political parties in the United States, such as the Green Party and the Libertarian Party. How do these parties differ in ideology? Do they hold the same values as they did when first formed?

Chapter 1
Rehearsal for Reconstruction

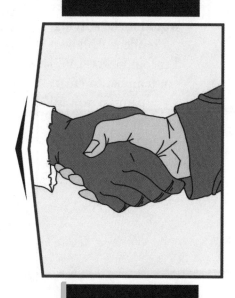

How did the final days of the Civil War set the stage for Reconstruction?

In the final years of war, politicians debated what the country would look like after the battles ended, when previously enslaved people would struggle to figure out how they would make a living.

President Abraham Lincoln (1809–1865) attempted to create a pathway toward equality, but his death complicated matters.

Even before the Civil War ended, experiments in Reconstruction began as emancipated slaves tested out their freedom and politicians debated proposals to reunite the country. By the summer of 1863, a Northern victory looked likely. While the armies fought for control on the ground, President Lincoln and the U.S. Congress battled over what post-war America would look like. Would freedpeople be compensated for the work they'd done without pay? Would ex-slave owners be compensated for the loss of their "property?"

How could the country come together again after years of trying to defeat the other side?

We can study these issues by looking at one region, an island where a grand experiment was being conducted in the name of politics.

THE PORT ROYAL EXPERIMENT

Port Royal, one of the Sea Islands off the coast of South Carolina, was a remote area of salt marsh, thick woods, and some of the most productive cotton plantations in the country. On November 7, 1861, an enslaved boy named Sam Mitchell grew afraid when he heard thunder boom in a cloudless sky. "Son, that ain't no thunder," his mother said. "That's Yankee, come to give you Freedom."

Only seven months into the Civil War, Union troops occupied the Sea Islands. White planters fled for the mainland, leaving behind 10,000 slaves. After destroying the hated cotton machinery, the liberated slaves divided up the land and began to plant corn and sweet potatoes to feed their families.

U.S. Treasury Secretary Salmon Chase (1808–1873) saw an opportunity on Port Royal. As an abolitionist, Chase wanted to prove that paid workers could produce cash crops as well as slaves could. As head of the U.S. Treasury, Chase also knew the government was almost broke and needed the money a Port Royal cotton crop would bring.

Port Royal, 1862

To achieve both objectives, Chase launched the Port Royal Experiment in the spring of 1862. The government hired former slaves to work in the cotton fields, established schools and hospitals staffed by missionaries from Northern aid societies, and set aside land freedpeople could purchase at a fair price.

EMANCIPATION PROCLAMATION

On January 1, 1863, President Lincoln issued the Emancipation Proclamation. This order freed enslaved people in the rebelling states and permitted African American men to join the military. However, slavery was still legal in Kentucky, Maryland, Delaware, and Missouri. Lincoln admitted the order was only a temporary war measure and a constitutional amendment would be needed to permanently end slavery. Why might a temporary measure be useful? Could the Emancipation Proclamation have negative effects?

The experiment had mixed success. Union soldiers, treasury officials, cotton investors, and missionaries often worked at cross purposes. When the laborers were paid late or less than expected, they refused to work. In April 1863, a group of women told their superintendent why they had walked off the fields. "We only wanted to know if we were sure of our pay. It is so hard living without clothes a whole year, and we get sick putting sea water in our hominy." The superintendent told the women if they refused to work, "the government would be disgusted with them," and let them come back.

Despite these problems, freedpeople did eventually purchase more than 30,000 acres of land in the Port Royal district. The experiment was an early effort at using land redistribution to allow former slaves a chance to get ahead economically.

THE 10-PERCENT PLAN

President Lincoln wanted a reconstruction plan to shorten the war, reunite the nation, and safeguard the liberty of former slaves. In 1863, he told Senator Zachariah Chandler (1813–1879) that he needed a strategy "firm enough not to go backward and yet not go forward fast enough to wreck the country's cause."

A group of African Americans on Port Royal Island, newly freed from slavery, c. 1863–1866

Credit: Hubbard & Mix, practical photographers

On December 8, 1863, Lincoln announced the Proclamation of Amnesty and Reconstruction, also called the 10-percent plan. After former Confederates swore an oath to the Constitution, Lincoln would grant them a "full pardon . . . with restoration of all . . . property, except . . . slaves." When 10 percent of the people who had voted in the 1860 presidential election had been pardoned, that state could form a new government and elect members to the U.S. Congress. Southern states could keep all their old laws—except slavery.

The 10-percent plan made no mention of civil or political rights for Blacks.

The Proclamation of Amnesty and Reconstruction received widespread approval. The *Chicago Tribune* wrote, "The political future begins to look clear." Northern Democrats were pleased because the plan would let stand most of the prewar laws of the South. Most Republicans were comforted by Lincoln's refusal to backtrack on emancipation.

However, African American leaders and their white Republican allies were furious. Former slave and abolitionist speaker Frederick Douglass (1818–1895) blasted President Lincoln. After asking Black men to fight for the Union, Douglass said, the president was now going to "hand the Negro back to the political power of his master, without a single element of strength to shield himself." Abolitionist Wendell Phillips (1811–1884), who was white, wrote that Lincoln's amnesty plan "makes the negro's freedom a mere sham" because the administration was "willing that the negro should be free" but sought "nothing else for him."

Read the 1865 letter from freedman Jourdan Anderson to his former owner at this website.

What is the tone of this document? How does Anderson answer his former owner's request for Anderson to work for him? How would you describe Jourdan Anderson's character based on this primary source?

digital history
Jourdan Anderson

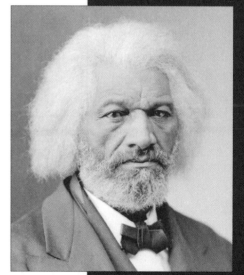

Frederick Douglass, between 1865–1880
Credit: Brady-Handy Photograph Collection

MANIFESTO

On August 5, 1864, Senator Wade and Rep. Davis responded to Lincoln's pocket veto in a manifesto. Describing the president as "dictatorial," they told him to "confine himself to his Executive duties—to obey and execute, not make the laws." But these lawmakers were out of step with the nation. Their manifesto was widely condemned. Lincoln claimed he had not read it, saying, "Time will show whether I am right or they are right." As you read on, decide for yourself whether President Lincoln did the right thing with his pocket veto.

Radical Republicans, led by U.S. Senator Benjamin Wade (1800–1871) and U.S. Representative Henry Winter Davis (1817–1865), struck back with their own reconstruction plan—the Wade-Davis Bill of July 1864. Central to this bill was the requirement that a majority of citizens of each state—not just 10 percent—must swear a loyalty oath to the United States before they could form a new government. Also, the rebel states must rewrite their state constitutions to abolish slavery.

Congress sent the bill to President Lincoln only minutes before legislators were scheduled to adjourn their session. Lincoln did not sign the bill, but neither did he veto it. This is known as a "pocket veto." By doing nothing, the president let the bill die when Congress adjourned.

On July 8, Lincoln issued a statement to explain why he had killed the bill. He did not want to reject the new governments that Arkansas and Louisiana had already established under his amnesty plan. Nor did Lincoln believe Congress had the constitutional authority to order states to abolish slavery. Instead, he was "sincerely hoping and expecting that a constitutional amendment, abolishing slavery through the nation, may be adopted."

THE THIRTEENTH AMENDMENT

On February 9, 1864, two Black men carried a petition with 100,000 signatures into the U.S. Senate chamber and set them on the desk of Massachusetts Senator Charles Sumner (1811–1874). For the past year, Sumner had been working on an amendment to abolish slavery. Now, he addressed the Senate. Finally, the Senate debate of the first constitutional amendment in 60 years began.

Senators argued whether it was fair to free enslaved people without compensating their owners. They discussed whether freed slaves should get more civil and economic rights. For most legislators, the goal was simply abolition. On April 8, 1864, the Senate passed the Thirteenth Amendment. But the amendment failed to pass in the House.

That summer, another 400,000 signatures supporting the amendment poured into the U.S. Capitol. In January 1865, the amendment was again introduced in the House.

This time, Lincoln exerted his presidential influence to sway the vote.

The pressure worked. On January 31, 1865, the Thirteenth Amendment passed the House of Representatives: "Neither slavery nor involuntary servitude, except as a punishment for crime whereof the party shall have been duly convicted, shall exist within the United States, or any place subject to their jurisdiction."

President Lincoln sent the amendment to the states for ratification. For an amendment to become part of the Constitution, three-fourths of the states must approve it. The Thirteenth Amendment passed that threshold on December 6, 1865.

SCENE IN THE HOUSE ON THE PASSAGE OF THE PROPOSITION TO AMEND THE CONSTITUTION, January 31, 1865.

A *Harper's Weekly* cartoon depicts the celebration in the U.S. House of Representatives after the adoption of the Thirteenth Amendment.

Credit: *Harper's Weekly*, February 18, 1865

NEXT STEPS

For some white activists, the abolition of slavery meant their fight for Black Americans was over. In May 1865, the president of the American Anti-Slavery Society, William Lloyd Garrison (1805–1879), said, "My vocation, as an abolitionist, thank God, is ended." He wanted the society dissolved. However, Frederick Douglass knew the end of slavery did not mean racial equality. "Slavery is not abolished," he told Garrison, "until the Black man has the ballot." But voting rights were not the top priority of legislators. They believed freedpeople had more immediate needs.

FORTY ACRES AND A MULE

On January 12, 1865, U.S. Secretary of War Edwin Stanton (1814–1869) and General William Tecumseh Sherman (1820–1891) met with 20 Black clergymen in Savannah, Georgia. Sherman's army had just conquered Confederates in Georgia, liberating 20,000 slaves along the way. Desperate for food, shelter, and protection, these men, women, and children attached themselves to the U.S. Army. But Sherman had a war to fight and no time for them.

So, Stanton asked the local Black leaders what freedmen most needed to support themselves. Garrison Frasier, a 67-year-old former slave, spoke for the group. "The way we can best take care of ourselves is to have land and turn it and till it by our own labor." Stanton ordered Sherman to draw up a plan to do just that.

On January 15, Sherman issued Special Field Order No. 15, setting aside 400,000 acres of confiscated land along the Carolina and Georgia coast for the use of liberated slaves. The land, called Sherman's Reservation, was divided into 40-acre parcels. Freedmen would be given first chance to purchase it before the government auctioned it off.

Mules no longer needed by the Union Army were also distributed to the freedmen.

Roughly 40,000 former slaves settled on Sherman's Reservation. However, the military gave them only "possessory titles," meaning they could work the land but did not legally own it. Overjoyed at having their own homesteads, the freedpeople did not realize that all too soon this land would be snatched away.

FREEDMEN'S BUREAU

In the spring of 1865, a fierce debate occurred in Washington, DC. With no money and no federal protection, how would freedmen survive in the South when the war ended? But was it the federal government's role to provide land, jobs, and education to former enslaved people when this assistance was not given to other Americans? Iowa Senator James Grimes (1816–1872) claimed, "Are they free men, or are they not? If they are free men, why not let them stand as free men?"

Senator Sumner countered that assistance was necessary as people transitioned from slavery to freedom. "The curse of slavery is still upon them," he insisted. Who do you think was right?

On March 3, 1865, Congress created the Bureau of Refugees, Freedmen, and Abandoned Land, called the Freedmen's Bureau. By law, the new agency would last only for one year after the war ended. Its mission was to provide food, clothing, and medical supplies to poor Southerners, establish schools, help negotiate employment contracts for freedpeople, and settle freedpeople on abandoned lands. Lincoln chose General Oliver Howard (1830–1909) to head the department.

Watch this brief video to learn about the amendment process.

Can the U.S. Constitution be changed? Other than through amendments, how has our Constitution kept up with the times?

Ⓟ
TED-Ed Constitution
Paccone

A man representing the Freedmen's Bureau stands between armed groups.

Credit: *Harper's Weekly*, July 25, 1868, A.R. Waud

THE FREEDMEN'S BUREAU.—Drawn by A. R. Waud.—[See Page 457.]

By the spring of 1865, Reconstruction was underway. The Thirteenth Amendment was working its way through the ratification process. Lincoln had decided on a lenient policy to readmit Southern states to the Union. The Freedmen's Bureau was ready to provide aid when the war ended.

The R. McLean House at Appomattox, in which General Lee surrendered to General Grant

Credit: The Major & Knapp Eng. Mfg. & Lith. Co. 71 Broadway

The Room in the McLean House, at Appomattox C.H., in which GEN. LEE surrendered to GEN. GRANT.

PEACE AT LAST

The end of the Civil War finally came on April 9, 1865, when U.S. General Robert E. Lee surrendered to Union General Ulysses S. Grant (1822–1885) at Appomattox, Virginia. Two days later, President Lincoln stepped out on a balcony of the White House to give the final speech of his life.

In Washington, DC, everyone was celebrating. American flags flew everywhere, and fireworks lit up the sky.

Spring rains had turned the streets into rivers of mud, but throngs of people stood outside the White House to hear the president. Lincoln said he hoped for "a righteous and speedy peace." He discussed the example of Louisiana, the first Southern state to hold new elections and adopt a constitution that abolished slavery. However, Louisiana's new government did not grant Black suffrage, and Lincoln said he thought educated freedmen and Black veterans should have the right to vote.

TEXT TO WORLD

Have you ever signed a petition to change a rule? Was the petition successful?

John Wilkes Booth leaning forward to shoot President Abraham Lincoln as he watches *Our American Cousin* at Ford's Theater in Washington, DC, 1865

Credit: based on the depiction from a mechanical glass slide by T.M. McAllister of New York, c. 1865–75

NOTHING LESS THAN THE WHITE MAN HAS

In October 1864, 150 African American leaders gathered in Syracuse, New York, for a four-day convention. These activists formed the National Equal Rights League and elected John Mercer Langston (1829–1897) to be the first chairman of what they hoped would become a permanent civil rights organization. The league called on the federal government to abolish slavery, guarantee equal rights for Black soldiers, and help freedmen acquire land and an education. Delegates did not think these things were too much to ask. During a keynote address, abolitionist John S. Rock (1825–1866) said that African Americans wanted only as much as "the white man; nothing more and nothing less."

Lincoln's statement about Black suffrage gave hope to African Americans that the president would not permit white planters to regain control of the South. They hoped that, with time, Lincoln would implement a Reconstruction plan based on racial equality.

But Lincoln was out of time. Four days later, the president was dead. And the man who replaced him proved to be no friend to African Americans.

KEY QUESTIONS

- Why did some lawmakers feel that leaving the question of voting rights for African Americans to the states was the right thing to do? What do you think?

- Which do you think was more important: finding ways of promoting equality for freedpeople or providing for basic survival, such as food and shelter?

BLACKOUT POETRY

Slavery tore families apart. Once liberated, former slaves immediately searched for missing family members, often through newspaper advertisements. You can read thousands of these nineteenth-century ads in online databases at these websites. In this activity, you will create a "blackout poem" by using a black marker to block out everything from an existing page of text except key words. The words you choose to leave visible create a poem.

Lost friends

Mother Bethel information wanted

VOCAB LAB

Write down what you think each word means. What root words can you find to help you? What does the context of the word tell you?

abolitionist, civil rights, compensate, manifesto, petition, suffrage, and **veto**

Compare your definitions with those of your friends or classmates. Did you all come up with the same meanings? Turn to the text and glossary if you need help.

- **Develop a list of questions about the people who wrote these ads.** How might such separations affect an individual, a family, and a culture?

- **Because these advertisements are so brief, you will have to infer their meaning based on evidence and reasoning.** What do you already know about slavery? What do you know about family relationships and loss?

- **Select several ads, print them, and tape them onto a single sheet of paper to create one body of text.** Read quickly over the ads, looking for words that connect directly or indirectly to your inferences. Circle these words in pencil. Read the circled words and make choices about which to keep visible and which to black out to create a message. Use a black marker to block out all the text except the words you selected for your poem.

- **Ask peers to read your poetry.** How do they react?

To investigate more, locate and read a newspaper story about immigrant families being separated at the U.S.-Mexico border. Considering the same questions you developed for enslaved families, create a blackout poem about separated immigrant families.

Chapter 2 ▶
Presidential Reconstruction

WILL THINGS EVER GET BETTER?

How was life during early Reconstruction different from life before the Civil War?

While the abolition of slavery was meant to improve the lives of Black people, white supremacists stayed in power and enacted the Black Codes, making life torturous for many freedpeople as they tried to work toward owning their own land, earning fair wages, and being politically active.

On April 14, 1865, President Lincoln was watching a play at Ford's Theater in Washington, DC, when actor John Wilkes Booth (1838–1865) snuck into the presidential box and shot Lincoln in the back of the head. Not only did this assassin's bullet rob President Lincoln of his life, it also propelled Vice President Andrew Johnson (1808–1875) into the presidency and the position of leader of Reconstruction.

Some congressmen believed Johnson would do a better job of reconstructing the South than Lincoln had managed. Shortly after Johnson took the oath of office, Senator Ben Wade and Rep. Henry Winter Davis met with the new president.

"Mr. Johnson, I thank God that you are here," Wade said. "Lincoln had too much of the milk of human kindness to deal with these damned rebels. Now they will be dealt with according to their deserts."

Johnson would soon prove Wade wrong.

JOHNSON'S PLAN

Americans expected President Johnson to take a hard line against the South and support equality for African Americans. In 1864, Johnson had told an audience of African Americans, "I will indeed be your Moses and lead you . . . to a fairer future of liberty and peace."

Congress was out of session when Johnson took over after Lincoln's death. That meant he had complete control over Reconstruction until lawmakers returned for their next session in late fall 1865. However, Republicans were confident Johnson shared their views on Reconstruction.

It was a shock **when the president revealed his lenient** Reconstruction plan **on May 29, 1865.**

Like Lincoln, Johnson promised amnesty to former Confederates once they took a loyalty oath to the United States. He also promised Southerners they would regain all their confiscated property—except their former slaves.

Thomas Nast cartoon about Johnson's reconstruction plan

RECONSTRUCT

When Senator Sumner met privately with the president, he urged Johnson to support giving freedmen the right to vote. Johnson reassured Sumner that "you and I are alike."

ANDREW JOHNSON'S BEGINNINGS

Andrew Johnson was born into poverty in North Carolina. As an adult, he opened a tailor's shop in Greenville, Tennessee, and entered politics. Johnson was a Democrat who championed the cause of the common man. He called wealthy plantation owners the "pampered, bloated, corrupted aristocracy." When Johnson became vice president in 1864, he was one of the most politically experienced men in the nation. He had been a U.S. congressman and governor of Tennessee and was serving in the U.S. Senate when the war began. When Tennessee seceded, Johnson refused to follow. By then a slaveowner, he freed his slaves, saying, "A loyal Negro is worth more than a disloyal white man." Keep Johnson's background in mind as we learn how he dealt with the huge project of Reconstruction. What attitudes from Johnson's background might have affected his actions?

The exceptions to Johnson's amnesty were high-ranking Confederate military officers, political leaders, and planters who owned more than $20,000. These men could receive a pardon only if they personally came before Johnson to request it. Having grown up poor in the South, Johnson resented the land-owning rich. As president, he held power over this social class and intended to use it.

President Andrew Johnson pardoning former Confederates at the White House.

Credit: Stanley Fox, *Harper's Weekly*, 1865

Republican lawmakers watched with dismay as upper-class Southerners flowed into the White House through the summer of 1865, walking out with presidential pardons.

By the fall, most former Confederates had their rights back.

The next phase of Johnson's Reconstruction plan was for Southern states to form new governments. Johnson appointed conservative Republicans and Democrats to serve as temporary governors to oversee this process. These governors held elections so Southerners could choose delegates to attend constitutional conventions. At these conventions, the delegates would rewrite state constitutions to obey federal law and ratify the Thirteenth Amendment.

However, President Johnson allowed the delegates to be elected according to the states' prewar constitutions. What did that mean? No Southern state allowed Black people to vote before the war. Therefore, no Black people could be elected as delegates and no Black people could attend the constitutional conventions to help draft the new constitutions. How could that be considered fair?

WHAT DID PEOPLE THINK?

Most Northerners supported the president's Reconstruction plan at first. Democrats liked the fact that Johnson was letting Southern states control their own affairs, which meant keeping whites in power. Many businessmen believed the president's approach would quickly revive Southern cotton production, meaning a better economy for all states. Conservative Republicans were satisfied because Johnson did not require Southern states to grant Black suffrage. They knew many white voters in their districts opposed Black people being allowed to vote.

However, many Republicans were alarmed by Johnson's plan. These Republicans were called the Radical Republicans, and their leader in the U.S. House of Representatives was Pennsylvania Congressman Thaddeus Stevens (1792–1868). He met with Johnson in May 1865 and asked him to hold off on carrying out Reconstruction until Congress returned to session. Johnson ignored this request.

In July, Stevens wrote to the president. He said many lawmakers feared Johnson's Reconstruction would "destroy the Republican party" and "greatly injure the country." He asked Johnson to call Congress back to Washington, DC, early for a special session. Again, the president ignored him.

Look closely at this 1865 political cartoon about President Johnson's pardons to former Confederates.

Does the cartoonist agree or disagree with what Johnson is doing?

Ⓟ
Pardon Franchise
Columbia

RECONSTRUCT

President Johnson used the U.S. Constitution to shield himself from criticism for allowing states to use their prewar constitutions when electing delegates, claiming it barred him from changing a state's voting rules.

In this political cartoon, illustrator Thomas Nash shows how things didn't really change for Black people after the Emancipation Proclamation.

Throughout the summer and fall of 1865, white Southerners rewrote their state constitutions and elected new lawmakers. Men who only months earlier had waged war against the federal government now won elections to serve in it. Even the former vice president of the Confederacy, Alexander Stephens (1812–1883), was elected to represent Georgia in the U.S. House of Representatives. What kinds of problems might this cause?

White Southerners went on to pass Black Codes to reestablish white supremacy. These laws replaced the slave codes that had been a part of the former state constitutions.

For example, in South Carolina, a Black man had to purchase a special license to work any job other than farmer or servant. Mississippi required Black men to show town officials proof that they had a job and home. In Louisiana, the head of Black households was required to sign a labor contract with a plantation each year, committing entire families to field labor. In Florida, Black people who resisted orders from a white person were labeled as vagrants and legally whipped.

View the 1865 Mississippi Black Codes at this website.

How did these laws limit the freedom of African Americans?

Black Codes Mississippi

SURGE OF VIOLENCE

With the Black Codes came a surge of violence. President Johnson sent journalist Carl Schurz (1829–1906) to travel through the South and assess the work of the Freedmen's Bureau. What Schurz discovered alarmed him.

White guerrilla units were terrorizing Southern Blacks. These men burst into freedmen's houses in the middle of the night. After yanking Black men and women from bed, the vigilantes beat them with clubs, whipped them with tree saplings, and sliced off their ears. Schurz reported that "Dead Negroes were found in considerable numbers in the country roads or on fields, shot to death, or strung on the limbs of trees." According to Freedmen's Bureau records, 1,000 Black people were murdered in Texas alone between 1865 and 1868.

The terrorists justified these murders with statements such as the victim would not "remove his hat" or "give up his whiskey flask" or "call her employer 'master'" or because he just "wanted to thin out the n----- a little." The killers were motivated by white supremacy. Southern whites could no longer legally own Blacks, but they refused to treat them as freedpeople.

> The Black Codes, designed to control freedpeople, were a continuation of the violence against Black people.

A visit from the KKK, 1872
Credit: Frank Bellew, *Harper's Weekly*, 1872

LAND GIVEN IS TAKEN BACK

The Freedmen's Bureau controlled 850,000 acres of land that had been either abandoned by Southern white owners or confiscated by the government. A key part of the bureau's mission was to settle freedpeople on their own farms. In July 1865, bureau commissioner General Oliver Otis Howard (1830–1909) authorized renting each family of freedpeople 40 acres of land for three years. After that time, the families would have the option to buy the land at a reasonable rate.

EDISTO ISLAND

In October 1865, 2,000 people gathered in a church on Edisto Island off the coast of South Carolina to hear what Freedmen's Bureau Commissioner Oliver Otis Howard had to say.

The freedpeople were frightened. They had been farming the island since their former owners had fled in the early days of the war. Rumors flew about the island, but no one knew the truth. Suddenly an old woman began to sing, "Nobody knows the trouble I've seen." Everyone joined in her lament. When the crowd fell silent, Howard confirmed the islanders' worst fears: President Johnson had ordered Edisto Island to be returned to its former owners. Howard recalled that with one voice, the people cried, "No! No!" The islanders appealed directly to President Johnson to let them keep their land. He never replied.

However, General Howard did not clear this move with President Johnson. Howard tried to get around Johnson's pledge to return all property to Southern whites by issuing an order to Freedmen's Bureau agents that stated, "The pardon of the President will *not* be understood to extend to the surrender of abandoned or confiscated property."

Believing just the opposite, on August 16, Johnson countermanded Howard's order. Southern whites who received pardons and paid all overdue taxes would get their land back. Johnson ordered Howard to tell the freedpeople that when the current crop was harvested, the land they were farming would be returned to its former owners. How might Black families, who thought they were finally at the beginning of independence, have felt?

Johnson's Reconstruction program was put into effect in the fall of 1865.

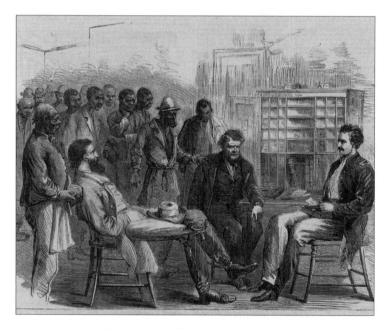

A meeting at the Memphis, Tennessee, Freedmen's Bureau, 1866

Soldiers forcibly removed freedpeople who did not sign labor contracts to work for their former owners. This included 20,000 freedmen in Virginia. In Louisiana, 62,000 acres farmed by Black people were returned to their former white owners. In Georgia and South Carolina, only about 2,000 freedmen managed to keep land the government had promised them.

"THE STUFF OF OUR GARDENS"

It was obvious that President Johnson was no Moses for freedpeople. The editor of the Cincinnati, Ohio's, *Colored Citizen* argued that Article IV of the Constitution guaranteed a democratic form of government in every state. Black Codes violated this, and so, the editor said, it was the federal government's duty to block the codes.

When whites in Georgia said their **Black Codes would teach freedmen the "arts of labor,"** the *Loyal Georgian* countered that former slaves have **had such training "all their lives."**

Individual freedmen took up their pens, too. A former slave begged the Union general overseeing Reconstruction in Tennessee for help. Former Confederates had ordered this man and the community of freedpeople he lived with to vacate the land they were living on. "There is almost a 100 family here on the north side of the river," the man wrote, "who was put here by the Government on land that people had gone and left . . . now those men has come back . . . and is going to turn us out of house and home and not give us time to gather the stuff of our gardens."

One man wrote to Senator Sumner that, "In most places the freedmen are worse off than when slaves, being exposed to the brutality and vindictiveness of their old masters."

RECONSTRUCT

Former Mississippi slave Merrimon Howard wrote that Black people had been left with "no land, no house, not so much as place to lay our head. Despised by the world, hated by the country that gives us birth, denied of all our writs as a people. . . ."

DON'T BANK ON IT

Now that freedpeople were receiving wages, they needed banks to deposit their money in. But white-owned banks would not do business with Black customers. In March 1865, the U.S. Congress chartered the Freedman's Savings and Trust Co. The bank's aim was to encourage freedpeople to be thrifty so they could escape poverty. The director and most trustees were white, but each branch hired Black clerks. Most customers opened accounts with less than $50. By 1873, the bank had 34 branches and held more than $3 million worth of deposits for more than 61,000 customers. However, when an economic depression struck the nation in 1873, the bank ran into financial trouble. On July 1, 1874, the bank shut down, and depositors lost all their hard-earned savings.

Some Black people were more militant. Major Martin Delaney (1812–1885) was one of the few Freedmen's Bureau agents who was Black. On July 23, 1865, he addressed 500 freedpeople in a church on Saint Helena Island, South Carolina. He urged them not to give up their land. "We have now 200,000 of our men well drilled in arms and used to warfare," Delaney told the crowd, "and I tell you it is with you and them that slavery shall not come back again."

Ultimately, bureau agents and freedpeople had little hope against the power of the Johnson administration. Agents encouraged freedmen to sign annual contracts and tried to negotiate the best wages they could on the freedmen's behalf.

RECONSTRUCT

Some threats of eviction were met with violence. Near Georgetown, South Carolina, white landowner William Bowl discovered his former slaves had moved into his mansion. He ordered them to leave, and they did—but first they burned his house down.

When the land they were promised was taken away, freedpeople were left with a deep sense of betrayal.

SUPPORT WEAKENS

Radical Republicans were alarmed by the support for Johnson's plan among Eastern cotton merchants, bankers, and Southern planters. During the summer and fall of 1865, they launched a campaign to convince Northerners that Black suffrage should be the next push now that slaves were free. They argued that without the vote, Black people would never be treated fairly in the South. However, the majority of Republicans believed lobbying for Black suffrage would divide the union more.

Yet, all Republicans and much of the Northern public were uneasy about other aspects of Johnson's reconstruction policies. They wanted life to return to normal, but they also wanted proof that Southerners accepted the consequences of losing the Civil War.

Throughout the fall of 1865, evidence from reporters, fact-finders, and private letters revealed that the attitudes and behaviors of Southern whites was not much changed from before the war.

President Johnson's Reconstruction was, as one New Yorker put it, "no reconstruction at all."

Reports of violence against freedpeople and the passage of Black Codes also reshaped the opinions of moderate Republican lawmakers. In mid-November, Congressman Schuyler Colfax (1823–1885) gave a speech in Washington, DC. He insisted that before Reconstruction was complete, the South must elect leaders who had not aided the Confederacy, and Southerners must "give evidence of their earnest and cheerful loyalty."

Most Republican lawmakers remained confident they could work with Johnson to modify Reconstruction, but those close to the president wondered.

This was the state of affairs when the 39th Congress reconvened on December 4, 1865. Could the U.S. Congress have an impact on the fate of Southern communities and the freedpeople who lived there? Was it too late to alter the path of Johnson's Reconstruction? Let's take a look in the next chapter.

Chicago editor Charles Dana (1819–1897) wrote in September 1865 that what frightened men in the North was "the idea that the rebels are all to be let back . . . and made a power in the government again, just as though there had been no rebellion."

KEY QUESTIONS

- How could the federal government both reunite the nation and offer justice to former enslaved people?
- How do the race relations of today reflect the relationships between Black and white people during the 1860s?

TEXT TO WORLD

Are there other countries where different regions have split apart and fought a war? How does a civil war affect ordinary people?

Inquire & Investigate

VOCAB LAB

Write down what you think each word means. What root words can you find to help you? What does the context of the word tell you?

amnesty, **Black Codes**, **conservative**, **freedpeople**, **moderate**, **pardon**, **rebel**, and **thrifty**

Compare your definitions with those of your friends or classmates. Did you all come up with the same meanings? Turn to the text and glossary if you need help.

PARDON ME

Article II of the U.S. Constitution gives the president the sole power to pardon someone. President Andrew Johnson used this power to pardon virtually all former Confederates who had waged war against the United States. How does Johnson's use of the pardon compare with that of recent U.S. presidents?

- **Develop a list of questions about how and when presidents use their power to pardon.**

- **Using books and reliable internet sources, research the answers to your questions about three of the following recent presidents:** Gerald Ford (1913–2006), Jimmy Carter (1924–), Ronald Reagan (1911–2004), George H. Bush (1924–2018), Bill Clinton (1946–), George W. Bush (1946–), Barack Obama (1961–), or Donald Trump (1946–).

- **Write a letter to one of these presidents.** Include evidence from your research about why you agree or disagree with how he exercised this authority.

> To investigate more, make a chart to compare and contrast the use of the pardon by Andrew Johnson and the presidents you researched. Based on these cases, why do presidents pardon people? Are the consequences of presidential pardons on society generally positive or negative? Are pardons a necessary presidential power or is it a power that should be removed from the Constitution?

Chapter 3 ▶
Congress Takes a Stand

I WILL SAY, HAVING FRIENDS THERE TO SUPPORT AND STAND WITH ME DID MAKE ME FEEL BETTER ABOUT THE SITUATION.

Why was there so much friction between the U.S. Congress and President Johnson?

Many Republican members of Congress disagreed with how President Johnson was managing Reconstruction. They wanted to see more support for African Americans. This conflict in ideals set the stage for fiery clashes in Washington, DC.

The 39th Congress reconvened on December 4, 1865. As the clerk of the House of Representatives called the roll, each representative responded. Then, the clerk reached the name of one of the newly elected representatives from the South—and skipped right over it. Shouts of protest erupted from the seats where Southern lawmakers sat. But the clerk kept reading the names, skipping over every single representative from the former Confederacy. This was no error. This was the Republicans' plan.

When the clerk reached the end of the roll call, a lawmaker from Tennessee demanded to speak. But Congressman Thaddeus Stevens said he refused to "yield the floor to any gentleman who does not belong to this body."

The House had the sole power to seat new members. If someone's name was not read in roll call, that person was not technically a member of Congress and could not vote on laws.

Regardless of President Johnson's lenient Reconstruction plan, Republican congressmen had no intention of allowing leaders of the former Confederacy to rise to power again.

Now that Congress was back in session, the House and Senate created a joint committee to investigate conditions in the South. They refused to allow the president to continue to control Reconstruction by himself. The power struggle between the executive and legislative branches had begun, and the fate of millions of freedpeople hung in the balance.

DIVISIONS WITHIN CONGRESS

Republicans controlled the 39th Congress, but they did not all agree on how to carry out Reconstruction. While they all believed freedpeople should have basic rights, they disagreed on what those rights were and what responsibility the federal government had in safeguarding those rights.

The lawmakers known as the Radical Republicans believed the moment had come for a second American revolution. Led by Pennsylvania Rep. Thaddeus Stevens in the House and Massachusetts Senator Charles Sumner in the Senate, the Radicals saw Reconstruction as a chance to reshape the United States so everyone was equal. They wanted to grant universal suffrage, meaning all citizens could vote. Also, the Radicals wanted to temporarily treat the former Confederacy as conquered territory with no rights, rather than as states. Article IV of the Constitution gave Congress the authority to govern conquered land.

THE GREAT COMMONER

Thaddeus Stevens was known as the "Great Commoner." In September 1865, Stevens gave a speech in which he pointed out that the 70,000 wealthiest former slave owners owned 394 million acres of land, which could be redistributed as 40 acres each to 1 million freedmen. The government would have land left over to sell to pay off war debts. When asked how the loss of land would affect the wealthy 70,000, Stevens said that for all he cared, those "proud, bloated, and defiant rebels" could go into exile.

Thaddeus Stevens between 1860 and 1875

Credit: Mathew Brady and Levin Corbin Handy

The Radicals believed they should control Reconstruction, not President Johnson. However, most congressional Republicans were moderates and viewed Reconstruction differently. Moderates considered Reconstruction a practical problem to be settled quickly. While some supported giving Black men the right to vote, they didn't speak out. They also agreed with President Johnson that, because secession was illegal, the Southern states had never really left the Union. By this reasoning, the states still had the powers given to them under the Constitution.

As soon as the 39th Congress opened, moderate Republicans rejected the proposals of the Radical Republicans and seized leadership of Congress. Senator John Sherman said the country had already "suffered too much from ultraists and wranglers"—in other words, people with extreme views.

Still, moderates were as **alarmed as Radicals about reports of violence against** freedpeople, the passage of **Black Codes, and the election of former Confederates. President** Johnson's Reconstruction **policies needed to be tweaked.**

President Andrew Johnson, c. 1875

Credit: Mathew Brady

Senator Lyman Trumbull met with Johnson at the end of December 1865 to explain the concerns of Congress. He left the meeting convinced that "the President wishes no issue with Congress and if our friends [the Radicals] would be reasonable we would all get along harmoniously." As 1865 ended, moderates hoped Reconstruction would go smoothly.

MODERATE REFORMS

Moderate Republicans believed two adjustments would fix the problems that stemmed from President Johnson's Reconstruction policies. They wanted to extend the Freedmen's Bureau and pass a civil rights bill. First, they tackled the bureau.

The Freedmen's Bureau was authorized to operate only one year beyond the end of the Civil War, and time was almost up. The agency was expensive to operate, but Republican lawmakers believed it did vital work. Also, Congress was still receiving alarming reports about violence against freedpeople.

Moderates wanted to extend the life of the bureau and give it more power.

Senator Trumbull drafted the new Freedmen's Bureau Bill and introduced it on January 5, 1866. The legislation would extend the life of the bureau until Congress abolished it and would authorize the president to reserve 3 million acres of unoccupied public land to be rented to freedpeople. The bill also stated that anyone who deprived citizens of their rights could be fined or jailed. After a three-week debate, the bill passed the Senate and was sent to the House, where it was expected to pass.

Then, Senator Trumbull got to work on a civil rights bill. His proposal defined all people born in the United States (except Native Americans living on tribal lands) as citizens and declared that, regardless of race, all citizens must receive "full and equal benefit of all laws and proceedings for the security of person and property."

View an anti-Freedmen's Bureau pamphlet on the Library of Congress website.

What methods does this pamphlet use to convince voters that the Freedmen's Bureau is not a good agency? Does this pamphlet seem racist to you? Why or why not?

Clymer Freedmen's Bureau

Senator Trumbull, between 1870 and 1880

Credit: Mathew Brady and Levin Corbin Handy

Moderate Republicans wanted freedpeople to be able to compete as free laborers in the South, something the Black Codes were blocking. To enforce this law, the bill empowered federal district attorneys, federal marshals, and Freedmen's Bureau officials to sue anyone, including local and state officials, who violated freedpeople's rights.

The civil rights bill that was introduced tried to define in legal terms what freedom meant in practical terms. The bill was not designed to protect just Southern Black people. Discriminatory laws in the North—and there were many—would also be invalidated. The bill passed both the House and Senate by March 15, 1866, and was sent to the president to sign.

RECONSTRUCT

The Freedmen's Bureau dispensed more than 13 million food rations throughout the South, including 4 million rations to poor whites.

AFRICAN AMERICANS CALL FOR REFORMS

While the Freedmen's Bureau bill sat on the president's desk and Congress crafted the civil rights bill, Black Americans seized the opportunity to push for more. They knew true equality required the power to vote.

In January 1866, delegates from 13 states gathered for the National Convention of Colored Men in Washington, DC. After much discussion, attendees decided to press the federal government to guarantee equal rights for all American citizens, "irrespective of race or color," including the right to vote. The convention statement mentions nothing about the right of women to vote, as female suffrage was not the primary concern. The convention selected five representatives to meet with President Johnson to state their case.

When the delegation entered the Oval Office on February 7, 1866, President Johnson was scowling. This was not a good sign. George Downing (1819–1903), a successful hotel owner, asked that African Americans be "fully enfranchised . . . throughout the land." Former slave and speaker Frederick Douglass said that since Black people paid taxes and fought for the country, they would like to "share in the privileges" of citizenship as well as its burdens. Douglass told the president that if given the vote, freedmen could ally with poor Southern whites to dismantle the power of the wealthy plantation owners. President Johnson was having none of it.

Johnson went on a long rant. Even though he had once owned slaves, the president claimed he had been a "friend of the colored man" all his life. Johnson then engaged in personal attacks. He said he did not like people who could "talk about abstract ideas of liberty, who never periled life, liberty, or property." This comment was cruelly ironic because Frederick Douglass had been beaten by a former slave owner, and his son, Lewis, who was also present, had been severely wounded in the Civil War.

Johnson told the delegation that he did not support Black suffrage.

Not only could it lead to a race war, but the president did not believe Black people would unite with poor whites if they got the ballot. Rather, he predicted, "The Negro will vote with the late master, whom he does not hate, rather than with the non-slaveholding white, whom he does hate." Johnson said the "majority" of people in each state had the right to decide who got the vote and who did not.

Maine Senator Lot M. Morrill (1813–1883) said, "This species of legislation is absolutely revolutionary. But are we not in the midst of a revolution?"

RECONSTRUCT

The president told his secretary, "Those damned sons of bitches thought they had me in a trap. I know that damned Douglass; he's just like any n-----, and would sooner cut a man's throat than not." What can you learn about Johnson's character from this statement?

In an open letter to President Johnson, a delegation of Black men dismantled key arguments Johnson had made against Black suffrage. The president had told the men that hatred between Black people and poor whites would continue even though slavery was abolished. If the president believed that, the men argued, he should immediately grant Black people the right to vote so they could protect themselves in such a hostile climate. "Peace between races," they wrote, "is not to be secured by degrading one race and exalting another, by giving power to one race and withholding it from another; but by maintaining a state of equal justice between all classes."

Read the entire letter at this website. What other arguments does the group make to counter President Johnson?

colored delegation
to president

At that moment, Frederick Douglass interrupted. He reminded the president that Black people *were* the majority in South Carolina and Mississippi. The president stood up. The meeting was over.

These delegates refused to give up. The men wrote an open letter to be published in the *Washington Chronicle*. They said Johnson's views were "entirely unsound and prejudicial" and they believed it was their duty to "expose . . . and, as far as may be in our power, arrest [Johnson's] dangerous influence." The president seethed.

VETO AND OVERRIDE

President Johnson contemplated the Freedmen's Bureau bill that lay on his desk. He had been hearing criticism about the bureau. When General Grant returned from a tour of the South, he told Johnson some Freedmen's Bureau agents were encouraging former slaves to have unrealistic expectations of what freedom might look like. General Dan Sickles (1819–1914), who was overseeing Reconstruction in Louisiana, claimed the bureau was full of "petty tyrants, knaves, and robbers, who were doing a great deal of harm." Johnson's cabinet believed the bureau cost too much.

With these complaints in mind, Johnson acted. On February 19, 1866, President Johnson vetoed the Freedmen's Bureau bill.

He explained that the bill was unconstitutional and unnecessary because the situation facing freedpeople was "not so bad."

Johnson rejected the entire mission of the bureau. Congress had never provided relief, built schools, or given land to "our own people," Johnson wrote. By this he meant white people. Johnson thought he should control Reconstruction because as president, he was the only official "chosen by the people of all of the states."

Johnson's veto stunned lawmakers. But it takes the votes of two-thirds of both houses of Congress to override a presidential veto, and Republicans could not manage this. They decided to revise the bill and hope Johnson would sign it in the future. Senator Fessenden, however, predicted that Johnson "will . . . veto every other bill we pass."

The civil rights bill was also waiting for Johnson's signature, and Republican lawmakers prepared for battle. An Ohio senator wrote to General Sherman, "If the President vetoes the Civil Rights bill, I believe we shall be obliged to draw our swords for a fight and throw away the scabbards." On March 26, Johnson vetoed the bill.

Johnson claimed the bill gave the federal government too much power. He believed that by helping Black people, the law discriminated against whites. "The distinction of race and color is . . . made to operate to favor of the colored and against the white race." The war was on.

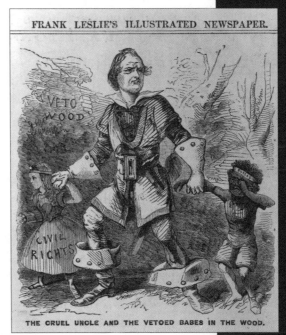

FRANK LESLIE'S ILLUSTRATED NEWSPAPER.

VETO WOOD

CIVIL RIGHTS

THE CRUEL UNCLE AND THE VETOED BABES IN THE WOOD.

DISRESPECT

Three days after he vetoed the Freedmen's Bureau bill, Johnson spoke at an event. When he mentioned enemies working to destroy the principles of American government, the crowd urged him to name them. "I say Thaddeus Stevens of Pennsylvania!" Johnson bellowed. "I say Mr. Sumner of the Senate is another." Even moderate Republicans were disgusted. Senator William Fessenden (1806–1869) wrote that Johnson had "broken the faith, betrayed his trust and must sink . . . into contempt."

The passing of the 1866 Civil Rights Act

Credit: Allyn Cox

On April 5, 1866, history was made when the Senate overrode the president's veto. A headline in one Republican newspaper bluntly revealed the state of the government: "The Separation Complete."

A fired-up Republican Congress took another stab at the Freedmen's Bureau bill and sent a revised bill to Johnson in early summer 1866. On July 16, he vetoed this version, too. But the Senate overrode his veto and the second Freedmen's Bureau bill became law.

Despite this pushback, President Johnson refused to yield ground. He kept pardoning Confederate leaders and taking land from freedpeople.

As Johnson and Congress played political tug of war, freedpeople faced an ever-rising tide of violence.

RECONSTRUCT

By the spring of 1866, the president had returned 414,652 acres of land to white planters, including 15,000 acres that had been given to freedpeople. Johnson also replaced Republican officials in the South with conservative Democrats who were uninterested in aiding freedpeople.

TEXT TO WORLD

Do you think today's U.S. government is as divided as it was during Reconstruction? Why or why not?

KEY QUESTIONS

- Who had a greater right to the land in the South, the former slaves who had worked the land or the white planters who had owned the land?

- What kind of Reconstruction plan could reconcile both groups' claims peacefully?

PATTERNS IN POWER

Inquire &
Investigate

Overriding a presidential veto was very rare in the nineteenth century. Is it still rare today? How has the power balance between the executive branch and the legislative branch evolved? Graph the presidential vetoes over the last century and look for patterns.

- **Use the internet to research the number of vetoes and veto overrides for presidents from 1920 to 2020.** Records are available on the websites of the U.S. House of Representatives and the U.S. Senate.

House Representative

- **Graph the data.** Which type of diagram will best represent the following variables: the number of vetoes of each president, the number of veto overrides for each president, the political party of each president? Consider a bar graph, line graph, frequency table, or circle graph. Which tool will best help you look for patterns through time? You can find a graphing tool here.

U.S. Senate

graphing tool

- **Analyze the data.** What patterns do you see? What is the relationship between presidential vetoes and veto overrides? What factors might explain the patterns you discovered?

To investigate more, research a president who vetoed many bills. What was going on domestically and internationally that might explain the opposition this president had to the laws the U.S. Congress wanted to pass?

VOCAB LAB

Write down what you think each word means. What root words can you find to help you? What does the context of the word tell you?

executive branch, **exile**, **legislative branch**, **override**, **racist**, and **veto**

Compare your definitions with those of your friends or classmates. Did you all come up with the same meanings? Turn to the text and glossary if you need help.

STORYBOARD THE CIVIL RIGHTS ACT OF 1866

A storyboard is a tool that directors use to describe key scenes in a film or TV show. It is a graphic organizer made up of a series of panels, each containing an illustrated scene and a written description. Create a storyboard to analyze the 1866 Civil Rights Act.

- **Write questions you have about the Civil Rights Act of 1866.** This will help you analyze the purpose and impact of this law.

- **Visit the library and use the internet to investigate answers to your questions.**

- **Create a storyboard template with as many panels as you need to analyze the law.** You can draw this template yourself or find one online. Label and illustrate each panel. Add dialogue, thought bubbles, and other text to explain each panel.

- **Compare your storyboard to those done by your friends or classmates.** How is your analysis of this law similar to and different from theirs?

To investigate more, do some research and complete a storyboard for the Civil Rights Act of 1875. Compare and contrast the two civil rights laws of the Reconstruction era. Which law was more effective in securing basic rights for African Americans and why?

Chapter 4 ▶
Radical Reconstruction

ALTHOUGH THERE HAVE BEEN MANY GREAT CHANGES IN OUR SOCIETY SINCE RECONSTRUCTION, THERE IS STILL A LOT OF WORK TO DO.

How did Congress and the president work together on Reconstruction?

President Johnson and the Radical Republicans who held power in Congress fought each other constantly about expanding the civil rights of African Americans. The two branches of government struggled at every turn.

A box arrived at Senator Charles Sumner's office during the debate over the 1866 civil rights bill. Sumner, an experienced lawmaker, was familiar with the ugly side of politics. Still, Sumner must have been shocked when he opened the box. It contained the severed finger of a Black person and a note that read, "You old son of a bitch, I send you a piece of one of your friends, and if that bill of yours passes I will have a piece of you."

The bill did become law and Sumner kept his body parts. However, Republicans knew the U.S. Supreme Court could declare the Civil Rights Act unconstitutional or a future Congress could repeal the law.

The best way to secure **freedpeople's rights was to embed them in the Constitution.**

THE FOURTEENTH AMENDMENT

Fear infected Congress throughout 1866. Fear that wealthy white landowners were regaining power in the South. Fear the South would once again dominate the federal government.

Since the Constitution was written in 1787, the political power of Southern states had been limited by the "three-fifths rule." This rule counted every five slaves as only three people in determining the population of a state. The state's population determined the number of representatives it could elect to the House.

However, now slavery was abolished. When Southern states were readmitted into the Union, African Americans would be fully counted as part of these states' population totals, and the South would gain many seats in the House of Representatives. But Black men were still prohibited from voting in the South. So, Republicans feared that by the 1870 election, Democrats would win control of Congress and the White House. Republicans worked frantically to reshape the Constitution before their fear could become reality.

After debating and rejecting dozens of proposals, Congress finally settled on an amendment they hoped would dismantle the power of former slave owners forever. It would not, however, establish the Black man's right to vote.

The Fourteenth Amendment established birthright citizenship. Anyone born or naturalized in the United States (except Native Americans) was considered a citizen.

NATIVE AMERICAN CITIZENSHIP

Native Americans were the first people to live in North America, but they were not granted U.S. citizenship until 1924. Under Article I of the Constitution, Native Americans who were not taxed were not considered citizens. In the nineteenth century, most Native Americans lived on untaxed tribal lands—therefore they were not granted U.S. citizenship. The Indian Citizenship Act of 1924 finally granted citizenship to all Native Americans. However, the right to vote was slow to follow. As late as 1948, Arizona and New Mexico still denied Native Americans the ballot. Why do you think this was the case?

RECONSTRUCT

The Fourteenth Amendment also prohibited states from depriving "any person of life, liberty, or property, without due process of law" or denying anyone "equal protection of the law."

Feminists had been campaigning for women's suffrage since 1848. When the movement's top leaders, Elizabeth Cady Stanton and Susan B. Anthony (1820–1906), learned that the Fourteenth Amendment addressed suffrage for only Black men, they launched a campaign for "universal suffrage." They called for all citizens, regardless of race or gender, to have the right to vote. On January 29, 1866, the group's first petition was read on the floor of the House. Hundreds more petitions would be delivered before women were finally granted the right to vote with the passage of the Nineteenth Amendment in 1920.

Read the wording of this petition at the National Archives. How do the authors try to persuade lawmakers to grant women the vote?

universal suffrage
petition constitution

The second clause in the Fourteenth Amendment reduced the threat of Democrats seizing control of Congress. A state's representation in Congress would be reduced by the number of "male citizens" who were prohibited from voting. White Southerners had a choice—either let Black men vote or lose representation. The amendment also barred top Confederate leaders—the very men President Johnson pardoned—from voting or holding office.

Not all Republicans were pleased with the Fourteenth Amendment. Some Radicals felt it did not go far enough because it did not directly give Black men the vote. For this reason, activist Wendell Phillips (1811–1884) called it a "fatal and total surrender." Feminists felt betrayed because the amendment mentioned only male citizens. Suffragette Elizabeth Cady Stanton (1815–1902) wrote, "If that word 'male' be inserted, it will take us a century at least to get it out."

A political cartoon showing the Democrats' view of the second clause of the Fourteenth Amendment, 1902

Credit: Edward Windsor Kemble

Despite these objections, the Fourteenth Amendment passed Congress. However, it would not become the law of the land until ratified by two-thirds of the states. Sadly, it took a massacre to rally support for ratification.

MASSACRE IN NEW ORLEANS

On July 30, 1866, 30 African American men walked to the Mechanic's Institute in downtown New Orleans, Louisiana. Whites were pressuring Republican Governor J. Madison Wells (1808–1899) to restore Louisiana's prewar constitution. Freedmen were upset about the state's Black Codes. The governor had called a convention, hoping to reach a compromise.

However, Mayor John Monroe (1822–1871), a former Confederate, vowed to stop the convention at the institute before it started. His tools to achieve this were the city police chief and his heavily armed force.

More than 150 Black people accompanied the 30 delegates as they walked to the Mechanic's Institute.

When the group reached Canal Street, police blocked its path. A scuffle broke out and a Black man was shot. The delegates took shelter inside the institute. Moments later, the police burst in, guns blazing.

The delegates tried to barricade themselves behind tables and chairs, but the police broke through these defenses. The few men who escaped into the street were chased and gunned down. By the time federal troops reached Mechanic's Hall, 47 Black men and one white man were dead. Another 116 people were wounded, including 16 police officers.

ANTHONY DOSTIE

A white Republican, Anthony Dostie (1821–1866), raised the American flag and tried to reassure the panicked crowd. "Keep quiet! We have here the emblem of the United States. They cannot fire upon us when we have this emblem." But the flag did not shield Dostie. His white skin probably inflamed the attackers. Some Southerners loathed white Northerners who had moved to the South to aid in reconstruction. A woman with the police yelled, "Those dirty Yankees were sent down here to destroy us! And those n------! Kill them!" The police shot Dostie.

The local military commander sent a report to General Grant describing the actions of the New Orleans police department as "murder." Mayor Monroe told President Johnson the delegates were rioters stirred up by white radicals, and he claimed 42 police officers were killed. Johnson accepted Monroe's version of events. None of the attackers were charged with a crime.

The Northern public was appalled at the violence and at Johnson's lack of response. *Nation* magazine wrote that what was most disturbing was "the coolness with which he [President Johnson] refrained from expressing one word of honest indignation at the slaughter . . . of unarmed men by a mob of their political opponents for political reasons."

Midterm elections were only weeks away. Northern voters had a choice—elect congressmen who supported President Johnson's policies or vote for change.

The riot in New Orleans

Credit: Theodore R. Davis, *Harper's Weekly*, 1866

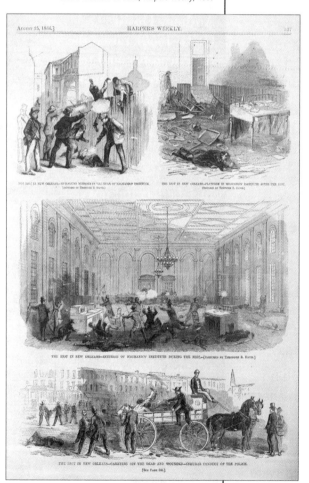

MIDTERM ELECTION 1866

Johnson hoped a sweeping victory by Democratic and conservative Republican legislators would let them seize control of Congress from the Radical Republicans. From August 28 to September 15, he embarked on a campaign tour called the "swing around the circle" to stir up support for his favorite candidates.

The tour was a fiasco. Johnson ridiculed members of Congress and got into shouting matches with audience members.

Even Johnson's supporters were appalled at the president's behavior. General Grant left the tour early, telling an aide he "did not wish to accompany a man who was deliberately digging his own grave." The *Journal of Commerce* described the president's behavior as "thoroughly reprehensible."

The 1866 midterm elections dealt a disastrous defeat to President Johnson's Reconstruction. Democrats lost 40 congressional seats while the Republicans gained 37. This gave Republicans a veto-proof majority in both the House and the Senate.

THE RECONSTRUCTION ACTS

The results of the 1866 election put the Radical Republicans firmly in control. *The New York Times* warned white Southerners to ratify the Fourteenth Amendment quickly or Congress would soon grant Black men the right to vote. The people of the South did not listen.

By the end of February 1867, **12 Southern legislatures had rejected the Fourteenth Amendment. Bolder laws were needed, but lawmakers were not sure how to best steer Reconstruction in a different direction.**

Then, Indiana Representative George W. Julian (1817–1899) suggested that lawmakers slow down. The South did not need "hasty restoration." Instead, Southern states needed "government, the strong arm of power, outstretched from the central authority here in Washington." Julian argued that the federal government should oversee the South for "some indefinite future time," until its society could be transformed.

In Cleveland, Ohio, when one man in the crowd called out that they should hang Jefferson Davis (1808–1889), the former Confederate president, Johnson replied, "Why not hang Thad Stevens?"

View the map of the 1866 congressional elections results at this website.

In what regions of the country was President Johnson's support the strongest? What explains why these regions backed Johnson's policies? How did the lack of representation in the South affect the election results?

USF map
congressional 1866

Lawmakers jumped on the idea. In early March 1867, Congress passed the Reconstruction Acts. These four interconnected laws divided the former Confederacy into five military districts.

U.S. Army generals would govern each district until acceptable state constitutions could be written and approved by Congress. All males, regardless of race but excluding former Confederate leaders, could participate in constitutional conventions to form the new governments. That meant former enslaved men—not former slave owners—would help draft the new constitutions. These constitutions were required to enfranchise Black men. Finally, before being readmitted to the Union, the states had to ratify the Fourteenth Amendment.

President Johnson was furious.
Johnson vetoed the Reconstruction Acts, but Congress overrode his veto.

The military was the key to enforcing the Reconstruction Acts, and as commander-in-chief, President Johnson controlled the military through his secretary of war, Edwin Stanton (1814–1869). However, Stanton supported most Republican policies, and Johnson wanted to fire him. But lawmakers did not want to lose their ally in the U.S. War Department just when they were going to implement the Reconstruction Acts.

To protect Stanton, Congress passed the Tenure of Office Act. It was a direct challenge to the executive branch. The Constitution gives the president the power to appoint his own cabinet members, but the Senate must approve these appointments.

A cartoon showing the Democratic view of the Reconstruction Acts, 1868

Credit: Thomas Nast

In an interview with the *New York Evening Post*, Johnson said the Reconstruction Acts would create chaos. He described white Southerners as "poor, quiet, unoffending, and harmless."

The Tenure of Office Act prevented the president from firing any official whose appointment required Senate approval unless he first received permission from Congress. To do so would be considered a "high misdemeanor," an impeachable offense.

RESULTS OF THE RECONSTRUCTION ACTS

Democrats fumed when the military took control in the South. One conservative New York editor wrote, "The [Negro] will be the master, the white man the slave, that or another rebellion."

However, African Americans welcomed the Reconstruction Acts as long overdue, and their lives improved quickly. Only one month after the acts were passed, the Freedmen's Bureau agent in Vicksburg, Mississippi, reported that local courts were treating freedpeople more fairly. The governor of South Carolina announced that his state would "cheerfully perform" the requirements Congress demanded. A former Confederate officer in Virginia published an open letter in which he urged whites to "recognize and respect the rights of the colored race."

African Americans embraced the Republican Party and held conventions across the South. The largest took place on April 2, 1867, in Savannah, Georgia, where 7,000 Blacks and whites vowed to "stand shoulder to shoulder in reorganizing our State Government." Tunis Campbell (1812–1891), a Freedmen's Bureau agent who had supervised land distribution in the Sea Islands, took the stage. Campbell called it a glorious day because "white and Black men had at last met under the old flag they loved so well to march to Union and victory." He was nominated to run for the Georgia state assembly.

THE UNION LEAGUE

Southern Black men received a political education from an organization called the Union League. The group was formed by Northern whites in 1862 to support Republican policies. After the war, the league, which was organized by mainly Black people, worked to build an alliance between the Republican Party and freedpeople. By March 1866, an estimated 2,000 Union League chapters were spread across the country. League members held voter registration drives and distributed political materials everywhere Black people gathered. One plantation manager said, "You never saw a people more excited on the subject of politics than are the negroes of the south. They are perfectly wild." Why might this have been true?

THOMAS ALLEN

Thomas Allen (dates unknown) was a freedman from Georgia and a shoemaker and preacher. What set him apart from other former slaves was that he was literate: "In my county the colored people came to me for instructions." Allen educated himself about political affairs by reading national newspapers, "I gave them the best instructions I could," he said. This leadership convinced local Blacks to elect Allen to the Georgia state legislature.

The Reconstruction Acts were the dawn of a new era. The military districts did what Southern authorities had refused to do. In Louisiana and Texas, General Philip Sheridan (1831–1888) ordered city mayors to hire Black veterans to staff half of their police forces. In the district that included Arkansas and Mississippi, General Edward Ord (1818–1883) prosecuted whites for assaulting Black people. Violence against freedpeople plummeted.

Black men were eager to exercise their right to vote, and they attended Republican Party conventions in each Southern state. Many of these men were originally from the North. Some had come South with the Union Army, while others worked for the Freedmen's Bureau or were teachers or ministers with Northern aid societies.

Former enslaved men also became political leaders. In 1867, 735,000 Black men registered to vote. However, Black people could not form the foundation of a strong Republican Party in the South on their own. Therefore, Black political leaders formed alliances with two groups of white Republicans.

Northern white men who moved to the South after the Civil War were called carpetbaggers. Most white Southerners viewed carpetbaggers with suspicion. They believed these men were trying to take advantage of the defeated South to get rich.

While some did move **south for economic opportunities, others were** idealists who wanted to **help former slaves.**

RECONSTRUCT

The term "carpetbagger" originated from the suitcases made from stitched rugs that some of these men carried. Many Northern migrants were lawyers, businessmen, editors, teachers, and former Union soldiers.

More important to the base of the Republican Party in the South were Southern-born white Republicans. These Southerners were called scalawags. The scalawags came from varied backgrounds. Some had supported the Union during the Civil War, but others had backed secession. Some were small-scale farmers, while others wanted to develop manufacturing in the South. What linked the scalawags was their belief that the South's future would be better served by Republican policies.

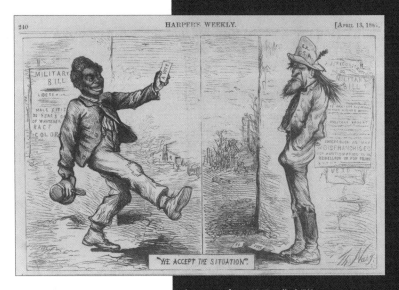

A cartoon from 1867 called "We accept the situation." Where is the irony in this illustration?

Credit: Thomas Nast, *Harper's Weekly*, 1967

Black Republicans, carpetbaggers, and scalawags did not agree on everything. Black people wanted land reform, while many whites were more interested in policies to help outside investors and Southern businessmen. Despite these differences, between 1867 and 1868, Southern Republicans elected biracial legislatures in Alabama, Arkansas, Florida, Georgia, Louisiana, North Carolina, and South Carolina. Lawmakers wrote progressive constitutions, ratified the Fourteenth Amendment, and rejoined the Union.

While this progress was happening at the state level, in Washington, DC, President Johnson refused to enforce laws that Congress passed. Finally, Republican legislators reached the end of their patience. It was time to bring Johnson to justice.

KEY QUESTIONS

- **How did the Reconstruction Acts aid in the ratification of the Fourteenth Amendment?**
- **How did Congress manage to control the executive branch of government when the two bodies did not agree?**

TEXT TO WORLD

Why is representation in government essential for equal rights? Can you think of any governments today that are misrepresenting the population?

THE IDEAL CITIZEN

Who gets to count themselves a member of a country's legal population? And how has America's perception of who deserves citizenship changed through time?

VOCAB LAB

Write down what you think each word means. What root words can you find to help you? What does the context of the word tell you?

biracial, carpetbagger, idealist, literate, progressive, repeal, and scalawag

Compare your definitions with those of your friends or classmates. Did you all come up with the same meanings? Turn to the text and glossary if you need help.

- **Draw an illustration of or describe an ideal citizen.** Consider what the ideal citizen believes, how the ideal citizen acts, what kind of people the ideal citizen hangs out with, and what the ideal citizen might say.

- **Work with a partner to research one of the following sets of laws or legal decisions.** Record how each either restricted or expanded who could be a U.S. citizen or resident.

Laws and court decisions that restricted citizenship:

- Nationality Act, 1790
- Alien & Sedition Acts, 1790
- *Dred Scott v. Sanford*, 1857
- Chinese Exclusion Act, 1882
- *Elk v. Wilkins*, 1884
- Expatriation Act, 1907
- Immigration Act, 1924.

- **Draw a new illustration of what the ideal American has been based on the laws you researched.** How does your new drawing compare with your partner's? What things do your drawings have in common and how are they different? What do the differences reveal about American society?

To investigate more, return to your original illustration. What changes in the law and in American attitudes must occur before your ideal citizen becomes the norm in the United States?

Chapter 5 ▶
High Crimes
and
Misdemeanors

How did Johnson's impeachment trial affect the lives of African Americans?

As the nation watched events unfold in Washington, DC, African Americans feared their treatment would worsen as white Southern leaders were emboldened to continue a legacy of racism and prejudice.

But the presidential election of 1868 gave them hope, especially as they turned out to vote for the first time.

The Radical Republicans in Congress wanted to continue to expand the rights of African Americans without having to fight the executive branch so often. President Johnson wanted to maintain control over Reconstruction and keep white people, including Confederate leaders, in power. How might these two goals be reconciled?

Could the power of one government branch be restricted so the other government branch had more freedom to act as it wanted?

Impeachment was high on the minds of the Radical Republicans. It was in the front President Johnson's mind, too.

HIGH CRIMES AND MISDEMEANORS

President Johnson believed Secretary of War Edwin Stanton had tricked him into executing a woman. In 1865, Johnson had signed the execution order for Mary Surratt (1823–1865) after a military commission convicted her of conspiring to assassinate President Lincoln. On July 7, Surratt was hanged. But on August 5, 1867, Johnson learned that five members of the commission that convicted her had signed a petition asking for the woman's life to be spared. Johnson never saw the petition. Convinced that Stanton had deliberately concealed it, Johnson decided the man must go. Besides—Stanton supported Reconstruction in the South.

But remember, the Tenure of Office Act prevented the president from firing Stanton without the consent of Congress. Because Congress was not in session, Johnson sent Stanton a note, telling the secretary his resignation would be accepted. Stanton ignored the request.

So, the president suspended Stanton, replacing him temporarily with General Grant. Stanton had expected such a move and accepted the suspension. But he made it clear that the Tenure of Office Act prevented Johnson from outright firing him.

President Johnson was angry. The president maintained his aggressive attitude in his annual message to Congress on December 7, 1867. His message was full of contempt for the Radicals' goal of universal suffrage. Johnson said, "Negroes have shown less capacity for government than any other race of people." What does this statement say about Johnson?

IMPEACHMENT 101

Presidents can be impeached and removed from office if found guilty of committing treason, bribery, or other high crimes and misdemeanors. This is the basic process Congress follows.

1. The House Judiciary Committee investigates the president's actions, holds a hearing, and, if convinced of evidence of misconduct, prepares articles of impeachment.

2. The House votes on whether to impeach (charge) the president.

3. If the majority of the House votes for impeachment, the president stands trial in the Senate.

4. During the trial, House managers serve as prosecutors, the president's lawyers mount a defense, and senators serve as impartial jurors.

5. For the president to be removed from office, two-thirds of the Senate must vote to convict on at least one impeachment article.

Like Mudds, Surratts Want Name Cleared

Ancestors doubt evidence in Lincoln slaying sufficient for hanging

Mary Surratt
'God knows I am innocent

By PAUL HODGE
The Washington Post

WASHINGTON — The Mudds and the Surratts, well-known names in Maryland's Prince George's and nearby counties for more than a century, have been trying for years to remove the stain on the family reputations caused by their ancestors' alleged part in the assassination of President Abraham Lincoln.

The Mudds were successful last month, when President Carter absolved Dr. Samuel Mudd of blame in the Lincoln conspiracy.

Now, County Executive Lawrence J. Hogan has issued a proclamation honoring Mudd and his 389 descendants, many of whom live in the county.

Descendants of Mary Surratt, convicted with Mudd in Lincoln's death — and hanged where Mudd was sentenced to life imprisonment — now are clamoring to have their family name cleared also.

Rep. Marjorie Holt (R-Md.) is studying proposals for legislation she hopes to introduce in Congress that would bring relief to the Surratt family, although what form the measure will take has not been determined.

Thelma Key Surratt Skinner, Mrs. Surratt's 80-year-old great-granddaughter, insists her ancestor's only guilt was by association. "My family has always thought it was an outrage . . . a military tribunal hanged a woman because she knew (John Wilkes) Booth," she said.

Skinner's family has lived in Baltimore since 1865, when the government convicted Mrs. Surratt and seven other "conspirators." At the time, the government confiscated Mrs. Surratt's house in Clinton, Md., then known as Surrattsville. Also confiscated was a boarding house she owned in Washington.

Ms. Skinner remembers talking to her grandfather, John Surratt, who plotted with Booth to kidnap Lincoln, but who was in Canada the night of the assassination.

Surratt was tried in 1867 by a civilian court, which heard virtually the same evidence and testimony upon which the military court convicted his mother. The civilian jury was unable to reach a verdict, and the charges against him were dropped later.

The Surratt family home was restored three years ago as a county historic park and now is headquarters of the Surratt Society.

Society president Laurie Verge said most of the members "are Lincoln assassination buffs and Surratt descendants who believe Mary Surratt was, if not completely innocent, at least was given an unfair trial."

There was no evidence to connect Mudd to the assassination conspiracy — except for his ministrations to the fleeing Booth.

Mudd was pardoned by President Andrew Johnson after four years in prison, ostensibly for his aid to fellow prisoners during an outbreak of yellow fever.

Mrs. Surratt's case was much more difficult. She was convicted primarily on the testimony of one of the conspirators, John Lloyd, an ex-Washington policeman and drunk who implicated her.

Lloyd testified that Mrs. Surratt told him to get the "shooting irons" and two bottles of whiskey ready to be picked up that night — indicating she knew of the guns at Surrattsville and of Booth's intention to kill Lincoln and then flee.

Booth was a frequent visitor to the Surratt boarding house, as were many of the other alleged conspirators, including Lewis Powell, who shot Secretary of State Seward while Booth was attacking Lincoln.

In his flight on horseback from Washington, after shooting the president, Booth stopped at the Surratt Tavern to get rifles an accomplice had stored there earlier and a package containing binoculars Mrs. Surratt had brought out from her city boarding house earlier that day. She later claimed that she did not know what was in the package.

Booth, wearing a disguise, then rode on to Mudd's home for treatment of his broken leg, which was injured when he jumped to the stage of Ford's Theater from the president's box. Mrs. Mudd commented that the man's beard appeared to be slipping and Mudd, when he learned of the assassination and the search for Booth, reported to soldiers that he had set the leg of a man who had come to him that night.

Dr. Samuel Mudd
absolved of blame by Carter

Mary Surratt's guilt is questioned to this day. This 1979 article from *The Atlanta Journal and Constitution* shows the family kept fighting for her to be declared innocent.

The House authorized the Judiciary Committee to investigate the president's "corrupt practices" regarding political appointments, pardons, and vetoes. When Congress returned to Washington in late November, legislators had to respond to Johnson's suspension of Secretary of War Stanton. The House Judiciary Committee recommended to the full House that the president be impeached.

However, moderate Republicans were not on board. The president had not fired Stanton, only suspended him. Moderate Republicans believed they could not impeach Johnson unless he clearly violated the law. When the full House voted on impeachment articles on December 7, 1867, the measure lost by a two-to-one margin.

> **This failure to impeach emboldened President Johnson. He walked right up to the line of impeachable behavior and deliberately stepped over it.**

JOHNSON FIRES SECRETARY OF WAR

It was a move by General Ulysses S. Grant that set the impeachment ball rolling again. Grant was disillusioned by serving in the Johnson administration. In January 1868, Grant quit his temporary post as secretary of war and turned the keys to the war office back to Edwin Stanton.

Friends advised Johnson to tolerate Stanton in his cabinet rather than fire him and violate the Tenure of Office Act. The president ignored them.

Johnson selected Adjutant General Lorenzo Thomas (1804–1875), a hard-drinking West Point graduate, to replace Grant. Thomas had sided with plantation owners opposed to freedpeople when he oversaw land claims in the Mississippi Valley during the Civil War. Stanton described Thomas as "only fit for presiding over a crypt of Egyptian mummies like himself." But Thomas would do Johnson's bidding until a permanent secretary of war was named.

Stanton had heard that Johnson was about to fire him and was prepared on February 21 when Thomas arrived at the U.S. War Department office with a dismissal note from the president. Stanton told his Radical allies in Congress what the president had done. Charles Sumner's advice was one word: "Stick."

With the support of most of Congress behind him, Stanton vowed to live in the war office 24 hours a day until the issue was resolved. A group of 100 congressmen gathered to protect him.

Copyright, 1891, by M. P. Rice, 1217-19-25 Penna. Avenue, Washington, D. C.

GENERAL U. S. GRANT.

From the only original unretouched negative, made in 1864, at the time he was commissioned by Abraham Lincoln Lieut. General of all the Armies of the Republic. It was suggested that this negative (with that of Abraham Lincoln) be made in commemoration of that event.

General Ulysses S. Grant, 1864

General Grant wrote to General Sherman about the Johnson administration that, "All the . . . feeling that man in high places . . . act only from motives of pure patriotism . . . has been destroyed."

IMPEACHED!

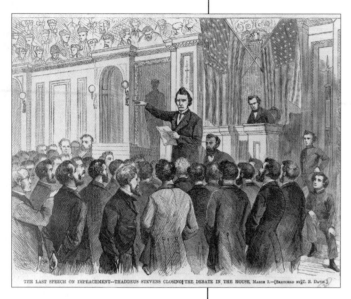

Thaddeus Stevens speaking to the House

Credit: Theodore R. Davis, *Harper's Weekly*, 1868

Watch this short video from *The New York Times* about how impeachment works.

What misconceptions do many people have about impeachment? What role does the Senate play in impeachment?

NYT impeachment video

As the House prepared to debate its response to the president's violation of the Tenure of Office Act, spectators packed the chamber gallery. At 2 p.m. on February 22, the full House began to debate whether to impeach President Johnson. Democratic Representative James Brooks (1810–1873) from New York called Stanton "arrogant, impertinent, and insolent" for refusing to resign. Brooks also said that 80 percent of the soldiers in the U.S. Army were loyal to Johnson. If the president was impeached, Brooks threatened, "We will never, never—so help me, God!—never submit."

But the Republican responses were just as sharp-edged. Congressman William D. Kelley (1814–1890) from Pennsylvania had personally witnessed racial violence in Alabama. "The unsheeted ghosts of the two thousand murdered negroes in Texas, cry . . . for the punishment of Andrew Johnson." The nation seemed on the brink of another civil war.

In the late afternoon of February 24, 1868, Representative Thaddeus Stevens took the House floor. Stevens was quite ill. He spoke in a slow, trembling voice and soon had to have the House clerk read his prepared speech. Stevens said lawmakers did not seek to impeach President Johnson because they disliked the president personally. Rather, if Congress shirked its constitutional obligation, the nation would become a "nest of shrinking, cowardly slaves."

Stevens meant that Congress was equal in power to the president, not below. The Constitution created three branches of government that share power. Johnson wanted to reconstruct the nation on his own, but he did not have that right. When Congress exercised its authority to pass laws, a president refusing to enforce them abused his authority.

The impeachment resolution passed on party lines: 126 yeas to 47 nays.

A committee of seven representatives wrote the articles of impeachment. Radicals wanted to throw the book at Johnson. But they relented to the demands of moderates that the impeachment remain focused on how the president actually broke the law. The committee drafted 11 articles of impeachment. Most related to Johnson's violation of the Tenure of Office Act, but one charge accused him of abuse of Congress.

THE TRIAL

On March 5, 1868, U.S. Supreme Court Chief Justice Salmon P. Chase (1808–1873) walked solemnly to the head of the Senate chamber and opened the impeachment trial of Andrew Johnson. Chase was not quite sure what he was doing—neither was anyone else. The Constitution does not provide guidelines on how to conduct an impeachment.

RECONSTRUCT

The procedures developed during Johnson's trial were put into the Senate's manual of operation. This manual was used by senators during the 1998 impeachment trial of President Bill Clinton and the 2020 trial of President Donald Trump.

WHAT IS IMPEACHABLE?

In 2019, the House of Representatives impeached President Donald Trump for obstruction of Congress and abuse of power. The president's defense attorneys used one of the same arguments President Johnson's lawyers used in 1868. Attorney Alan Dershowitz (1938–) said Trump could not be convicted on an impeachment charge unless he committed a crime. Dershowitz explained, "Purely noncriminal conduct including abuse of power and obstruction of Congress are outside the range of impeachable offenses." The Constitution states that presidents could be impeached for "high crimes and misdemeanors;" however, these terms are not specifically defined. So, Congress must define them for each impeachment. How might this lead to different standards being used for different people?

Without a clear plan for how to run an impeachment, the 54 senators figured things out as they went along. The House managers insisted that the impeachment trial was not a criminal trial. They did not need to prove the president was guilty beyond reasonable doubt. Impeachment, they argued, was a political process concerned with a president's fitness for office or abuse of power, rather than whether he had committed an actual crime.

The Senate did rule that President Johnson did not have to appear as a witness. Johnson's lawyers had lobbied hard for this. Johnson was well-known for his scrappy nature and fondness for calling his enemies names. His lawyers would speak for him.

Audience members in the gallery of the Senate during the impeachment trial of Andrew Johnson

Credit: W.S.L. Lewett, *Harper's Weekly*, 1868

When opening statements were finally delivered on March 30, the nation was riveted. So many spectators wanted to watch the proceedings that the Senate distributed 1,000 tickets each day of the trial to control the flow. House manager Benjamin Butler (1818–1893) rose to present the prosecution's opening statement. Once a formidable courtroom attorney, Butler was known to be a dynamic speaker. The chambers hushed. Senators leaned forward in their seats. Spectators in the gallery leaned forward in their seats.

Not this time. Instead, Butler clutched a sheaf of papers in his hand and delivered a somber argument packed with legal citations that sent some listeners into a stupor. In the weeks since the House had impeached Johnson, tempers had cooled.

Radicals believed their best chance at securing a conviction was to present a rational, legal argument that Johnson had violated the Tenure of Office Act. But by the end of his opening statement, Butler was back to passionate form. He said that Johnson was "the elect of an assassin" who only became president because of "a foul murder," and, therefore, he really was not even a legitimate leader. Harsh words!

President Johnson was defended by five attorneys. Their argument was that Johnson had not violated the Tenure of Office Act because Stanton had actually been appointed by President Lincoln. Therefore, Johnson was not required to keep a former president's cabinet member on the job.

For two long months, the trial proceeded. A total of 25 prosecution and 16 defense witnesses testified.

Moderate Republicans from states that bordered the South feared that if they voted to convict the president, voters might punish them in the fall elections.

On May 16, 1868, the Senate cast its first vote. Johnson needed to be convicted on only one of the 11 articles to be removed from office, but a conviction required two-thirds of the senators.

During the trial, President Johnson kept a low profile. He abandoned his usual insult-laden speeches and instead spoke privately to senators. He promised to stop interfering with congressional legislation and to appoint a respectable person as secretary of war if they did not vote to convict him.

Left to right: (seated) Benjamin F. Butler, Thaddeus Stevens, Thomas Williams, John A. Bingham; (standing) James F. Wilson, George S. Boutwell, John A. Logan

Credit: Mathew Brady

San Francisco editor Philip A. Bell (1808–1889) complained that the Republican Party called itself a reform party. He wrote, that when lawmakers finally prove that Johnson was guilty ". . . and his conviction would restore peace . . ., we find Republican Senators . . . standing in the way of the reform which his removal would produce."

TEXT TO WORLD

Did you follow President Trump's impeachment trials in 2019 and 2021? How did they compare to Johnson's?

The senators first voted on Article 11, a sort of catch-all charge that summed up the other 10 articles. Seven moderate Republicans voted with Democrats and the vote was one short of the two-thirds needed for a conviction.

The Senate voted next on the firing of Secretary of War Stanton. The same seven Republicans voted with the Democrats and the result was the same. Johnson was acquitted by one vote.

The writing was on the wall. The moderate Republicans were not going to convict President Johnson. James Grimes (1816–1872), one of those moderates, explained his reason. "I cannot agree to destroy the harmonious working of the Constitution for the sake of getting rid of an unacceptable president." There was no point in continuing. The Senate voted to halt the impeachment trial.

African Americans were crushed. Not only was President Johnson going to remain in office, but the fact that some Republicans had allied with Democrats worried them. After the passage of the Fourteenth Amendment, Black people had finally begun to trust that the Republican Party was serious about racial equality. Now, they were not sure.

But African Americans still had cause for hope. The presidential election of 1868 was only a few months away, and General Ulysses S. Grant, the general who had led the North to victory in the Civil War, was the Republican nominee for president.

ELECTION OF 1868

Although African Americans could not vote in most of the North, thanks to the Fourteenth Amendment, Black men in the South could vote for president. Black people knew how critical this election was.

One California woman said she had not bought new clothes for months because, "If Grant was not elected, she would never want anything more to wear, for she would die."

Grant defeated the Democratic nominee, New York Governor Horatio Seymour (1810–1886). His victory in the popular vote was only five percentage points, closer than people had expected. However, Grant won the electoral vote by a landslide: 214 to 80, thanks to the 400,000 Black men who voted for him.

White people inflicted a lot of violence against Black voters in the lead-up to the election. Once the results were in, however, white Democrats seemed to rethink their situation. One Nevada man said, "We should no longer sanction the bloody deeds. Let us no longer press the Negro and deny him a home in the land that gave him birth."

The *New Orleans Democrat* agreed. The paper wrote that white violence had "driven Blacks into the Republican ranks and fenced them in there." If Southerners wanted Democrats back in power, they had to appeal to Black voters.

While Democrats did some soul searching, African Americans prepared to finally take their place as full citizens. Publisher Philip A. Bell said Grant's election was even more important than Lincoln's: It "firmly establishes the Reconstruction Acts . . . and shadows forth the speedy accomplishment of equal suffrage for all citizens." It was the dawn of a new day.

VOCAB LAB

Write down what you think each word means. What root words can you find to help you? What does the context of the word tell you?

acquit, **bribery**, **disillusioned**, **impartial**, **impeach**, **prejudice**, and **treason**

Compare your definitions with those of your friends or classmates. Did you all come up with the same meanings? Turn to the text and glossary if you need help.

KEY QUESTIONS

- **Do you think Johnson's impeachment trial was fair? Why or why not?**

- **How effective is the impeachment in checking the powers of the executive branch?**

EVALUATING MEDIA BIAS

The media plays a major role in shaping public opinion, especially about controversial topics. Because a democracy depends on a well-informed public to hold government accountable, citizens must know how to evaluate the media in order to detect potential bias. Evaluate news sources about the impeachment of President Donald Trump in December 2019.

- **Use the internet to locate three articles about Trump's impeachment.** Select articles from Fox, MSNBC, and the Associated Press.

- **As you read the three articles, record the following information in a chart: media name, author, date, main argument, and two facts that support the main argument.**

- **Assess each source for its reliability and accuracy.** Crosscheck the facts in each article by looking for confirmation or rejection of these facts in other sources. Examine the background of the author—are they a professional journalist, a politician, or have some expertise that makes them qualified to report on this issue? What is the point of view of the article and is it one-sided? What is the purpose of the article and who was its intended audience? What information does the source leave out that would help you better understand Trump's impeachment?

- **Evaluate the articles.** Based on your analysis, which of the three media sources do you think presents the most balanced, factual, unbiased viewpoint of Trump's impeachment?

To investigate more, locate other types of sources about Trump's impeachment, such as news videos, blogs, or interviews. How do these sources explain Trump's impeachment and how do they compare with the coverage of the three articles you read?

Chapter 6 ▶
A Moment in the Sun

How did African American lives change after the election of President Grant?

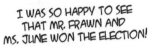

From education and financial independence to political careers, African American lives improved—for the most part.

On February 23, 1870, Hiram Revels (1827–1901) entered the Senate chambers to be sworn in as senator from Mississippi. The last man to represent Mississippi in the U.S. Senate was Jefferson Davis. Nine years earlier, Davis had left the Senate to become the president of the Confederacy. Now Revels, an African American Republican, would take his seat.

The election of Hiram Revels **represented the expansion of equality achieved during the peak of Reconstruction.**

Now, despite the resistance from white Southerners and President Johnson, freedpeople gained new political power. They developed institutions that became the foundations of the modern Black community in the South.

THE ROAD TO THE FIFTEENTH AMENDMENT

Although Black men were able to vote in the South after the Reconstruction Acts of 1867, most Northern states still barred Black men from the polls. Northern voters did not seem inclined to change this. The North's reluctance to give the vote to Black men shows that white racism was not just a Southern problem. Northern whites may have supported the abolition of slavery, but that did not mean they supported racial equality.

In New York, for example, Black men could vote only if they owned at least $250 in property. Some 21,000 Black men lived in New York in 1867, but only 2 percent owned enough property to meet this requirement. New York's Republican governor urged the state assembly to abolish the rule. But when the measure came up for a vote in the spring of 1867, moderate Republicans joined Democrats to defeat it.

That same year, citizens in Ohio, Kansas, and Michigan rejected measures to enfranchise Black men. In the border states of Kentucky, Delaware, Missouri, and Maryland, lawmakers did not even propose suffrage bills. African Americans knew the best way forward was through a constitutional amendment.

In January 1869, representatives from 21 states met in Washington, DC, for the National Convention of the Colored Men of America. The delegates agreed that although freedpeople in the South had many pressing concerns, "The question of suffrage was paramount at the present hour."

NOT A CITIZEN?

Democratic senators refused to recognize Hiram Revels when he was elected to the Senate in 1870. According to the Constitution, a senator must have been a citizen for at least nine years. The Dred Scott decision of 1857 ruled that African Americans were not citizens. This ruling was overturned by the Fourteenth Amendment. Democrats, however, insisted Revels did not qualify because the amendment was not ratified until 1868. They argued that he had been a citizen for only two years. After three days of heated debate, the Senate finally voted to recognize Revels.

U.S. Senator Hiram Revels, the first African American in the U.S. Congress, between 1860 and 1875

Credit: Mathew Brady and Levin Corbin Handy

RECOGNIZE THE WOMAN

When the Pennsylvania delegation arrived at the 1869 National Convention of the Colored Men of America, one of them was a woman. Miss H.C. Johnson was the second woman ever to attend a colored convention. Some men objected to Johnson's presence. Fields Cook (c. 1817–1897) from Virginia said he had thought "the call for this convention to be expressly for colored men." But Johnson had defenders too. H.J. Brown, the delegate from Maryland, wanted women to know that they were living in "a progressive age, and that women would yet have a vote." Finally, the attendees voted, and Johnson won. This one Black woman joined the convention for Black men. What does this incident show about discrimination throughout history?

On February 5, convention president George Downing (1819–1903) sent a petition to Congress. The writers reminded Congress that Black people were citizens and it was the government's primary duty to protect its citizens.

> Without the vote, Black people were **"unprotected . . . at the mercy of the country . . . a despised class."**

Radical Republican congressmen agreed that a constitutional amendment was needed to guarantee universal male suffrage. However, many were less motivated by the desire to grant Black men the right to vote than were worried because the Democratic Party had gained ground in the elections of 1867 and 1868. A constitutional amendment that enfranchised Black men in the North and protected the vote of Black men in the South would secure the national power of the Republican Party.

RECONSTRUCT

During the debate about the Fifteenth Amendment, a rift opened between Black men and white women, former allies in the suffrage movement.

Feminist leader Elizabeth Cady Stanton was furious that the amendment did not grant women the right to vote. On January 19, 1869, during a meeting of the American Equal Rights Association, Stanton used racist language when she condemned the amendment.

Stanton said that women could scarcely bear being oppressed by their own fathers, but now, under this amendment, they would be oppressed by men far beneath them.

"Think of Patrick and Sambo and Hans and Yung Tung," Stanton said, clumping Irish, Black, European, and Asian men together, "who do not know the difference between a monarchy and a republic, who can not read the Declaration of Independence or Webster's spelling-book," making laws for educated suffragettes like her and other middle-class white women.

Frederick Douglass, a long-time supporter of women's suffrage, countered Stanton's logic: "When women, because they are women, are dragged from their houses and hung upon lamp-posts; when their children are torn from their arms, and their brains dashed upon the pavement . . . when they are in danger of having their homes burnt down over their heads . . . then they will have an urgency to obtain the ballot equal to our own."

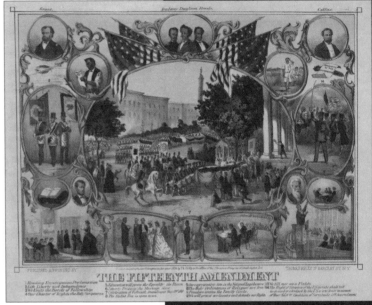

Celebrations of the Fifteenth Amendment
Credit: Thomas Kelly

But Stanton refused to accept Douglass's argument. She walked out of the meeting and went on to form a separate organization, the National Women's Suffrage Association.

At the end of February 1869, Congress passed the Fifteenth Amendment. The wording was simple: "The right of citizens of the United States to vote could not be denied on account of race, color, or previous condition of servitude." As the amendment headed to the states for ratification, President Grant stated that the adoption of the amendment "completes the greatest civil change, and constitutes the most important event that has occurred, since the nation came into life."

The first African American senator and representatives Robert C. De Large, Jefferson H. Long, Hiram Revels, Benjamin S. Turner, Josiah T. Walls, Joseph H. Rainy, and R. Brown Elliot

Credit: Currier & Ives, 1872

Go to the chart of Black officeholders in the South on the Facing History website.

In which states were most Black men elected? What might account for this?

Facing History Black officeholders

In March 1870, Georgia became the 28th state to ratify the amendment, and Black people across the nation celebrated. More than 10,000 marched in Baltimore, Maryland. In Los Angeles, California, the artillery fired a 100-gun salute. Frederick Douglass gave an address in Albany, New York, and he said, "The Black man is free, the Black man is a citizen, the Black man is enfranchised . . . no more a despised and hated creature, but a man. And what's more, a man among men."

With the vote came political change. Few Black men were elected to political office in the North because most African Americans lived in the South. However, with the passage of the Fifteenth Amendment, Black men won elections to all levels of government throughout the former Confederacy and in Missouri and Washington, DC. The most significant change was in South Carolina, where 316 Black men held state office, with a majority of the state legislature.

This level of participation was not seen everywhere. In Tennessee, only 20 Black men were elected to state office between 1868 and 1876, and Missouri elected only one. On average, fewer than 20 percent of Southern political offices were held by Black men during Reconstruction.

REPUBLICANS IN POWER

Hostile newspaper editors were convinced that Black lawmakers would care only about Black voters. A Florida journalist reported that Black Republicans in his state had pledged not to help anyone "who had voluntarily been in the Rebel Army."

This did not happen. Republican state governments worked to reform all aspects of society. State-funded public schools were established in the South at this time, as were orphanages and hospitals for the mentally ill. South Carolina and Texas made school attendance compulsory. In South Carolina, lawmakers expanded the property rights of married women, funded medical care for the poor, protected minors against abusive parents, and held white fathers financially responsible for any mixed-race children.

Nashville, Tennessee, provided food and firewood to the homeless. Petersburg, Virginia, paved dirt streets and established a board of health.

These reforms benefitted everyone, not just Black people.

EDUCATION

Before slavery was abolished, every Southern state except Tennessee made it a crime to teach enslaved people to read and write. As a result, 90 percent of the Southern adult Black population was illiterate. But the desire to learn was strong, and with emancipation came opportunity. Freedpeople also needed to learn for practical purposes. As they entered the workforce, Black people needed to be able to read documents such as land deeds and labor contracts.

FARM TO CLASSROOM

Elijah Marrs (1840–1910), a freedman and Union veteran from Kentucky, returned to his state and began to farm. As one of the few literate Blacks in Simpsonville, Kentucky, he was urged to teach. Marrs did not feel qualified, but he decided to "leave the corn-field and enter the school-room to labor for the development of his race." Marrs taught 150 students.

Sewing class at the Haines Normal and Industrial Institute, Augusta, Georgia

NOT EVERYONE IS HAPPY

Schools and teachers were often targeted by angry Southern whites. When female teachers walked down the streets, they were told to "go to the devil." Male teachers were run out of town, beaten, and even killed.

In 1866, whites in North Carolina set fire to four Black schools in less than three months, and Freedmen's Bureau agents in Texas reported that "school houses were burnt nearly as fast as they could be erected." Until the Reconstruction Act sent troops into the South in 1867, white arsonists engaged in almost nightly assaults on bureau schools.

During Reconstruction, funding for Black schools was provided by Northern charities, the Freedmen's Bureau, and Southern state governments.

However, the motivation for learning came from freedpeople themselves.

The first wave of teachers consisted mostly of white, middle-class, Northern missionaries. But in places where no Northern teachers were available, freedpeople took on the role of teacher. The superintendent of the Freedmen's Bureau schools, John Alvord (1807–1880), described "native schools," where former slaves became teachers, some of them having just learned to read themselves.

Black people who lived in urban areas set up schools in churches, abandoned warehouses, pool halls, or the basements of private homes. In New Orleans and Savannah, schools were erected on the grounds of former slave markets. Children were seen teaching their parents the alphabet, and laborers read books during their lunch breaks.

Because funds from the Freedmen's Bureau were never enough, Black people funded their own schools as best they could. Former slaves in San Antonio, Texas, taxed themselves between 50 cents and a dollar so they could purchase a schoolhouse. Freedmen in Charleston purchased books and formed a library association so people who could not afford to buy books could still read them. Boys chopped firewood to heat rural school buildings and girls collected pine resin to light lamps.

When Alvord toured the South in the spring of 1866, he found 1,405 teachers working in 975 schools. Altogether, 90,778 students were enrolled in 15 Southern states and the District of Columbia.

These figures did not include the many small schools operated without aid from the Freedmen's Bureau. By 1870, Black people in the South had spent more than $1 million on education. What does this say about their values?

By the fall of 1869, Freedmen's Bureau schools enrolled 256,834 Black students. Northern aid societies founded the South's first Black universities of Fisk, Hampton, and Tougaloo. By the turn of the century, the illiteracy rate among Southern Blacks had plunged to 50 percent from 90 percent in 1860.

BEGINNING OF SHARECROPPING

When President Johnson ordered all confiscated and abandoned land returned to pardoned Confederates, the freedpeople who were living on that property were given the choice to either work for their former owners or move. Most had little choice but to remain as sharecroppers.

Cotton farming in Mississippi, 1898

In this system, individual families signed contracts with landowners to work a specific plot of land. Usually, the landowner provided the family with tools, fertilizer, seed, and plow animals. Then, at harvest, the sharecroppers kept one-third of the year's crop and gave the rest to the owner.

Sharecropping had advantages for landlords and tenants. Freedpeople had the flexibility to control their own schedules. Landowners could depend on a stable workforce because sharecroppers had an incentive to stick around until harvest to reap the benefits of their labor.

Sharecropping did not, however, provide the economic freedom former slaves wanted.

Too often, the system trapped Black families in a cycle of poverty. During the year, they might have to borrow money from the landowner for medicine, clothing, or food. Then, at the end of a hard year's work, the owner would deduct this debt from the freedmen's share of the harvest.

TEXT TO WORLD

How has your education helped you so far? What difference has it made in your life?

Sometimes, families found they owed the landowner money rather than the other way around. This was especially true as cotton prices continued to fall.

Despite sharecropping's drawbacks, it had its successes. A Freedmen's Bureau agent described a female sharecropper from Talladega, Alabama. She worked a small patch of cotton and earned $98. The woman said, "I plowed, and I sowed, and I hoed every lick of it myself, and I picked it, and got it baled and sold it too." This woman was not unique. Some worked while their husbands attended school or political conventions. They were motivated to earn money so their children could attend school and have a better future.

Some freedpeople managed to claim land of their own. Others just moved onto unused land. Others found sympathetic whites willing to sell them land. A group of Black people in Hampton, Virginia, pooled their money and bought several hundred acres of land. They named it Lincoln's Land Association and farmed it together.

While the return of confiscated land to white Southerners did limit the number of freedpeople who became landowners during Reconstruction, Black people still gained some economic freedom. When the Civil War began in 1861, no Southern Blacks owned their own land. By 1880, 20 percent did.

Political empowerment, educational access, and the right to control their own labor—these were the new freedoms African Americans gained as Reconstruction peaked in the early 1870s. These gains did not last. By the mid-1870s, the Reconstruction era reforms were being steadily destroyed.

BLACK CHURCHES

Before emancipation, enslaved people had to attend churches run by white people. Slaves were forced to sit in the balcony or the back of the church. During Reconstruction, Blacks left these white congregations, pooled their resources, and built their own churches. These African American churches became the core of Black communities. They were used as schools as well as for social gatherings. Connections made in church led Blacks to form fire departments, debate clubs, and drama societies. Churches were centers for political organization, and more than 100 Black preachers held elected office during Reconstruction.

KEY QUESTIONS

- Why is economic independence such a major part of freedom and equality?
- Why is education so important on the path to equality?

CONTRACT NEGOTIATIONS

Who had the upper hand in sharecropping contracts—the landowner or the laborer? Examine an 1868 contract to figure out the answer.

- **Go to the Alabama Department of Archives and History.** Locate the 1868 contract between 16 freedmen and landowner H.W. Whipple.

🔎 archives Alabama Whipple

- **Analyze the terms of the contract.** What services will the freedmen provide? What compensation will they receive? What non-labor expectations for both the landlord and laborers are spelled out in the contract?

- **Calculate the pay.** Look at the wage rates for the highest- and lowest-paid laborers listed. Based on the terms of the contract, roughly how many hours must they work per day? How much would their hourly rate be? How much would their annual income be?

- **Evaluate the contract.** Which party do you think is getting the better deal in this contract, the landowner or the freedmen? How can you tell?

> To investigate more, locate a website that provides historic prices for goods and services. Make a budget for one of the sharecroppers. Based on the price of food, clothing, and housing in 1868, how difficult would it be for this worker to survive financially on these wages?

Chapter 7

The Wheel of Progress Rolls Backward

HATE CRIMES ON THE RISE AS FEAR OF THE CORONAVIRUS GROWS AND UNEMPLOYMENT HITS AN ALL TIME HIGH . . ..

Why did Reconstruction end as it did?

The Democratic Party gained the upper hand in many states as their citizens turned their attention toward the lagging economy and the presidential election sealed the fate of racial equality for the next several decades. African Americans realized that while slavery may have been outlawed, social justice was receding.

Slavery was abolished. The Fourteenth Amendment granted birthright citizenship. Black men had the right to vote. Southern states were once again part of the Union. Many white Republicans considered Reconstruction complete. In April 1870, *New-York Tribune* editor Horace Greeley (1811–1872) expressed the feeling of many Northerners in a bold headline: "Let us have done with Reconstruction. The country is tired and sick of it."

This was a sign that the counterrevolution had begun. As Northern whites turned their attention away from Reconstruction, Southern whites unleashed a barrage of violence designed to force freedpeople into the role of second-class citizens.

Many people might have considered Reconstruction to be over, but for African Americans in the South, daily life was full of reminders that equality had not been achieved.

POLITICAL VIOLENCE

Freedmen were supposed to be able to safeguard their own rights once they had the power to vote. But in the run-up to the 1868 election, Southern Democrats used intimidation and violence to keep Black people from the polls.

The Ku Klux Klan, a paramilitary group founded in 1865, was the most notorious terrorist group. Klan members targeted activists and lawmakers, freedmen and white Republicans. Before the presidential election in 1868, the Klan killed about 1,000 people in the South.

One out of every 10 Black men who had been a delegate to the Southern constitutional conventions was either murdered or wounded by these domestic terrorists.

In response to this political violence, Congress passed a series of laws between 1870 and 1871 called the Enforcement Acts. The first act banned people from going "in disguise upon the public highways, or upon the premises of another" in order to violate someone's civil rights. The second act, passed in February of 1871, empowered federal judges and marshals to supervise local polling places. The third Enforcement Act, known as the Ku Klux Klan Act, authorized the president to use the U.S. Army to arrest anyone who violated the civil rights of freedpeople.

THE KU KLUX KLAN

The Klan was founded by former Confederates in 1865. General Nathan Bedford Forrest (1821–1877) was the group's first "grand dragon," or national leader. Members took an oath to work for white supremacy. According to Union General Benjamin Butler, if the Klan could not achieve its goals through the political system, it would resort to "force, fraud, and murder." Members wore hoods with eye slits, hoping to frighten Black people into thinking they were the ghosts of dead Confederate soldiers.

But no one was fooled. "Spite dey [their] sheets and things," former slave Lorenza Ezell (1850–unknown) said, "I knowed dey voices." Ezell knew who his assailants were because Klansmen were his neighbors.

Credit: Lorenza Ezell

Thomas Nast, *Harper's Weekly*, 1874

Through the summer and fall of 1871, the U.S. Justice Department began to prosecute Klan members in Southern states. By then, the violence in South Carolina was out of control. On October 17, President Grant sent federal troops into nine South Carolina counties to arrest people. In one county alone, 195 Klansmen were arrested, 200 fled, and another 500 turned themselves in.

The Enforcement Acts made a difference.

The Justice Department convicted 168 people before interracial juries. These criminals received lengthy prison sentences in Northern prisons. The tough enforcement broke the back of the Klan. Frederick Douglass said, "Peace has come to many places as never before. The scourging and slaughter of our people have so far ceased."

RECONSTRUCT

Although 97 white men were arrested and charged with violating the Enforcement Act in the Colfax Massacre, only a handful were convicted.

Yet, other paramilitary organizations filled the void left by the Klan. The White League, the Red Shirts, and the Knights of the White Camilla shared the same goal as the Klan— white supremacy. The White League carried out one of the worst incidents of racial violence during Reconstruction, the Colfax Massacre of 1873.

Republicans narrowly won the 1872 Louisiana governor's race in a hotly contested election, and Democrats vowed revenge. In the spring of 1873, white Democrats in Colfax County, Louisiana, called for armed supporters to help them oust Black and white Republican officials. To defend these leaders, an all-Black militia occupied the courthouse. On April 13, 1873, more than 150 former Confederate soldiers and members of the White League attacked the courthouse. Historians estimate between 60 to 150 Black men were shot or hanged in the Colfax Massacre.

Death at the Polls
Credit: Thomas Nast, *Harper's Weekly,* 1879

Those charged and convicted appealed the verdict, and the case traveled all the way to the U.S. Supreme Court. In 1876, the high court overturned the convictions. Why? According to the justices, the Fourteenth Amendment only empowered the federal government to stop state governments from committing civil rights violations. If individuals, such as the White Leaguers, deprived a freedman of his civil rights, the federal government had no authority or jurisdiction. It was up to local or state authorities to charge these criminals. Too often, these officials themselves were the perpetrators of the violence.

THE REDEMPTION

Southern whites wanted to re-establish white supremacy in the former Confederacy and called this effort "Redemption." The redeemers were white Southern Democrats, and their main goal was to neutralize the Black vote.

(PS)

In 1871, Congress launched an investigation into the extent of Ku Klux Klan violence throughout the South. The following year, Congress held public hearings in which victims and perpetrators testified about their experiences.

Go to this website to find excerpts of some testimony from these hearings. What impact might this type of violence have on the turnout of Black voters on election day?

testimony of
Harriet Postle

Ninety percent of all African Americans lived in the South at the time, and Blacks made up a majority of the population of South Carolina, Mississippi, and Louisiana. South Carolina was a state that redeemers considered a prime example of the threat posed when African Americans voted. Black men dominated the state legislature and had been elected lieutenant governor, secretary of state, and treasurer, and to the state Supreme Court. Redeemers wanted to crush Black political power in South Carolina and throughout the former Confederacy.

The first step of the Redemption movement was to regain Southern state governments by discouraging Black voters from going to the polls. Southern whites accomplished this through economic intimidation. For example, a white landowner would threaten to evict a Black sharecropper if he dared to vote in an upcoming election.

If the threat of homelessness did not work, then a visit from the Klan or the White League was usually enough to terrorize Black voters into staying home on election day. Then, once Democrats had regained political power, white lawmakers rolled back rules that had benefited freedpeople.

Beginning in the early 1870s, Blacks began to see their rights erode in one Southern state after another. Kentucky banned Blacks from testifying in court. Delaware business owners were allowed to refuse admission to anyone who customers considered "offensive." After Democrats seized control of South Carolina's state government in the 1876 election, the legislature closed the state's integrated university and then reopened it to whites only.

RECONSTRUCT

In one Alabama county in 1870, a Black woman was brutally beaten by a group of white men. The Democratic judge refused to hear her case until she paid a $16.45 fee. The woman paid the fee, but then the judge released her attackers and told her to drop the complaint or he would put her in jail.

Northern whites had no time to worry about the concerns of Southern Blacks when their own economic survival was at stake.

The Grant administration was so plagued by scandals that the executive branch paid little attention to how the South was violating freedpeople's rights. Corruption was rampant. Wall Street financiers tried to control the gold supply. The Union Pacific railroad paid off congressmen. Although Grant was reelected in 1872, investigations of these scandals and media attention consumed the administration. To make matters worse, the economy began to fall in 1873.

ECONOMIC DEPRESSION

Railroad construction had been booming since the end of the Civil War. Between 1866 and 1873, more than 35,000 new miles of track were laid. Companies invested heavily in the railroad industry—often too heavily. In September 1873, the Jay Cooke and Co. Bank did not have enough money to cover its customers' deposits, so it closed its doors. Quickly, the economic dominoes began to fall.

Dozens of banks and brokerage houses went bankrupt. The stock market was temporarily closed. Eighty-nine railroad companies collapsed. By 1876, 14 percent of Americans were unemployed and 18,000 businesses had failed. Factory workers' wages fell 50 percent in two years.

The depression of the 1870s hit the South even harder than the North. Between 1872 and 1877, the price of cotton fell almost 50 percent. Tobacco, rice, and sugar also dropped steeply. Small farms were hit hard. As the value of their crops plummeted, both white and Black landowners could not pay their debts at harvest time. Banks foreclosed on their land and these farmers became sharecroppers to survive.

A Tennessee newspaper interpreted the results of the 1874 election as a condemnation of Reconstruction: "This recent election was not an election. It was a country coming to a halt and changing front. The whole scheme of Reconstruction stands before the country today a naked, confessed, stupendous failure."

Unemployed rioters in New York, 1874

Credit: *Frank Leslie's Illustrated Newspaper*, 1874

THE CAPSTONE OF LIBERTY

In January 1874, South Carolina Congressman Robert B. Elliot (1842–1884) urged his colleagues to pass the proposed Civil Rights Act. He said, "This bill will determine the civil status, not only of the negro, but of any other class of citizens who may feel themselves discriminated against," as Black spectators packed the House gallery. Elliot compared America's democracy to a piece of architecture. The civil rights bill would be "the cap-stone of that temple of liberty . . . a building the grandest which the world has ever seen." When he concluded, spectators gave him a standing ovation.

RECONSTRUCT

The Civil Rights Act of 1875 was revolutionary but rarely enforced. White business owners believed the law violated their rights to operate a business how they saw fit.

The depression turned political in 1874, when voters turned on the Republican Party. The House flipped from a Republican majority of 110 representatives to a Democratic majority of 60. Democrats also gained control of the Senate, won governorships in 23 states, and held majorities in 23 state legislatures, including in the North.

THE CIVIL RIGHTS ACT OF 1875

Senator Charles Sumner was getting old and his health was failing, but he was still a man on a mission. In 1870, Sumner introduced a bill to ban segregation in public places, including theaters, churches, schools, and cemeteries, as well as in jury selection. The goal was to establish social equality between Blacks and whites. The bill created an uproar and failed to pass.

But the law's supporters did not give up. On March 11, 1874, Charles Sumner died. On his deathbed, Sumner had pleaded with his colleagues to "take care of my civil rights bill." The version of the bill that finally became law on March 1, 1875, did not contain the requirement for racially integrated schools and cemeteries. But it did grant Americans equal access to inns, public transportation, and places of entertainment, regardless of race or color.

In 1883, five cases involving Black people who were denied equal access to public places were heard by the U.S. Supreme Court. In what were called the "Civil Rights Cases," the Supreme Court declared the Civil Rights Act of 1875 unconstitutional. The justices ruled the Fourteenth Amendment prohibited discrimination by only the states, not individuals. Black Americans would have to wait 74 years for the next civil rights law.

COMPROMISE OF 1877

A secret deal in a smoke-filled hotel room is what many historians identify as the event that ended Reconstruction once and for all. The deal was a result of the presidential election of 1876. Democrats nominated New York Governor Samuel J. Tilden (1814–1886), a man who had tackled political corruption in his state. Republicans selected Rutherford B. Hayes (1822–1893), a Union veteran, former congressman, and three-time governor of Ohio.

Credit: Thomas Nast, *Harper's Weekly*, 1877

The lead-up to the election was violent. Black people endangered their lives if they went to the polls.

In South Carolina, former Confederate General Martin Gary (1831–1881) encouraged "every Democrat . . . to control the vote of at least one negro, by intimidation, purchase, [or] keeping him away." If that meant killing the voter, so be it. "A dead Radical is very harmless," Gary wrote.

On November 7, 1876, roughly 82 percent of registered voters cast their votes for president, but it would be almost four months before Americans knew who won. When the votes were counted, Tilden carried four Northern states and every Southern state except the three that Republicans still controlled—South Carolina, Louisiana, and Florida. There was so much violence and fraud in those states that the results were unclear. Hayes won the rest of the North and much of the West.

According to the Pew Research Center, 64.1 percent of all eligible Americans voted in the 2016 election. However, Black turnout fell for the first time in 20 years in a presidential election. In 2012, 66.6 percent of African Americans voted. But in 2016, only 59.6 percent went to the polls.

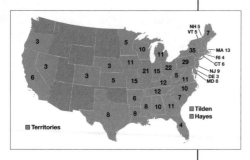

The 1876 Electoral College results

Tilden won the popular vote. Without the 19 electoral votes from South Carolina, Louisiana, and Florida counted, the results of the Electoral College were 165 for Hayes and 184 for Tilden. The House established an electoral commission to review the results in the three disputed states. It was made up of five Republicans, five Democrats, and five Supreme Court justices. Three of the justices were Republicans.

By a vote of eight to seven, the commission declared Hayes the victor in the three disputed states. This gave him 185 electoral votes, one more than Tilden, and just enough to win.

> Democrats did not **accept defeat. This is where the secret deal in the smoke-filled** room became part of the story.

On February 26, 1877, five Ohio Republicans and four Southern Democrats met in the Wormley Hotel and hashed out the Compromise of 1877. Democrats agreed not to fight Hayes's election as president in return for some concessions. In addition to federal funding for Southern projects, the Democrats demanded they be allowed to retake political power in Louisiana, South Carolina, and Florida. The Republicans agreed.

After Hayes took office, the editor of the *Nation* magazine predicted, "The negro will disappear now from the field of national politics. Henceforth, the nation . . . will have nothing more to do with him."

On March 3, 1877, Rutherford B. Hayes was sworn in during a private ceremony in the White House. Hayes told advisers and friends that his policy would be to leave the South alone. Reconstruction—an era when Republicans controlled Southern politics, Black people had broad political power, and the federal government was responsible for protecting the rights of Black citizens—was over.

THE TRANSITION TO JIM CROW

Change did not come to the South overnight. Black men could still vote and hold elected office in many areas after 1877. For several years, African Americans were still admitted to theaters, bars, and hotels and could choose their own seats on street cars and trains in some communities.

However, the wheel of progress was rolling backward. By the 1890s, Southern states were drafting new constitutions. Lawmakers worked around the Fifteenth Amendment by requiring voters to pay a poll tax or pass a literacy test in order to vote.

These barriers, as well as violence, disenfranchised Black people all over again. Brave individuals still challenged the power of white supremacy that denied them their constitutional rights, but these activists lacked political power.

In one of his final speeches, Frederick Douglass addressed a Washington, DC, audience on January 9, 1894. The aged leader summarized what was happening in America. "When the moral sense of a nation begins to decline and the wheel of progress to roll backward, there is no telling how low the one will fall or where the other may stop." Then, he posed a question, "We may well ask what is next."

What came next were decades of legal segregation called the Jim Crow system. This was paired with violence and an intensive effort by white Southerners to shape the national memory of both the Civil War and Reconstruction.

The last Black congressman from the South at that time was George White (1852–1918) from North Carolina. He left office in 1901. No other African American from the former Confederacy would serve in Congress until Barbara Jordan (1936–1996) from Texas was elected in 1968.

KEY QUESTIONS

- **How should a democratic society respond to political violence and terror?**
- **How can individuals respond to political violence and terror?**

TEXT TO WORLD

Have you ever felt scared or intimidated to do something? How did you handle it? Did anyone help you?

HARD HISTORY

Between the Civil War and World War II, thousands of African Americans were lynched. This means they were murdered by white mobs. These acts of racial terrorism were a method whites used to control Black people. It is an ugly side of American history that is not often taught in school. Experts believe that until Americans recognize the history of racial terror and how it led to inequality, we cannot address the racial divisions that still plague society today.

Work with a group of peers to create a series of infographics about the history of lynching, from the end of the Reconstruction era to the 1950s.

- **Develop a series of questions to guide your research.** Divide these questions among your group so each person's infographic focuses on a different question.

- **Visit the library and research on the internet to answer your questions.** Remember to evaluate your sources to make sure they are trustworthy. Two valuable websites include Lynching in America and State Sanctioned. **NOTE: These websites may include disturbing images.**

lynching America

state sanctioned

- **Determine the purpose of data you want to display.** Here are some tips. Use large colorful fonts and icons to display statistics or facts. Use charts or pictograms to show similarities or differences. Use a line graph, timeline, or thematic map.

- **Design your infographic.** Use a digital template or create your own from scratch.

To investigate more, present your infographic to a group of social studies teachers, parents, or the school board. Do they think the history of lynching should be taught as part of American history?

Chapter 8 ▶
The Legacies of Reconstruction

What can today's society learn from Reconstruction's aftermath?

Rewriting history through books, movies, and other forms of propaganda is a way of erasing the forward strides made by people who worked hard to achieve some level of success. As the story of Reconstruction was altered to justify widespread racism, the truth became murky, and it wasn't until a new civil rights movement began that people began to again accept reality.

Wars are not waged just with guns. Propaganda, ideas, and images are also powerful weapons. In the late nineteenth century, white Southerners used these tools to reshape the national memory about the Civil War and Reconstruction. They were successful, and this distortion of history still echoes through the present.

In 1866, Edward Pollard (1832–1872), a Virginia newspaper editor, wrote *The Lost Cause: A New Southern History of the War of the Confederates*. In the book he laid the groundwork for what became the widely accepted myth known as the "Lost Cause."

The Lost Cause had three core beliefs. First was the fiction that before the war, the South was a paradise populated by kind-hearted masters and contented slaves. Pollard described slavery as "one of the mildest and most magnificent systems of servitude in the world."

In 1881, former Confederate President Jefferson Davis added to the myth when he published *The Rise and Fall of the Confederate Government*. Davis claimed that slavery transformed Black people "from a few unprofitable savages to millions of efficient Christian laborers."

The second belief of the Lost Cause was that the South did not secede over slavery. Jefferson Davis wrote, "The existence of African servitude was in nowise the cause of the conflict." Instead, proponents of the Lost Cause claimed, the South seceded because the federal government was violating the Constitution by interfering in their affairs. When the North invaded the Confederacy, the argument went, Southerners had to defend themselves.

The final belief of the Lost Cause was that the Confederate Army was composed of heroes who always acted honorably. These rebels did not lose the war because they were not skilled warriors or lacked will, but because the North outgunned and outmanned them. The Lost Cause glorified and romanticized the Confederate Army.

Why do you think people wanted to believe these fictions?

The Lost Cause, 1869

Credit: Henry Mosler

REWRITING HISTORY

The 1906 textbook, *The Child's History of North Carolina*, has a chapter on the Ku Klux Klan. You can read it here.

How does this textbook portray the actions of the Klan during Reconstruction? How does this portrayal compare with what you have learned in this book? How can you determine which record is accurate?

Hathi *A Child's History of North Carolina*

This sanitized version of the past took root when white Southerners founded Confederate patriotic societies. The United Confederate Veterans (UCV) was established in 1889. The organization held annual gatherings of former Confederate veterans. At its first convention in 1890, members declared their mission was to "demonstrate esteem and admiration for the courage of Confederate soldiers while some were still alive." By 1904, the UCV had more than 80,000 members.

These veterans wanted to ensure they would be remembered by future generations. In 1890, the Sons of Confederate Veterans was formed, followed by the United Daughters of the Confederacy. In 1892, the UCV created a committee to promote the teaching of "proper" history about the Civil War and Reconstruction. Committee members scrutinized textbooks, weeding out those that "slandered" the South by suggesting the Confederacy had fought to preserve slavery.

Many white historians approved of *The Lost Cause*. One of these was William A. Dunning (1857–1922). The "Dunning School" of thought taught that Reconstruction failed because Black people were incapable of managing their new rights.

PUSHING BACK

Black Americans did not sit idly by as their achievements and characters were condemned. Intellectuals such as Mississippi Congressman John Roy Lynch (1847–1939) and Harvard-educated author and professor W.E.B. Du Bois (1868–1963) struck back at white historians who were playing fast and loose with the facts.

W.E.B. Du Bois, 1904

Credit: James Purdy

Lynch published a book titled *The Facts of Reconstruction*. In it, he laid the blame for Reconstruction's failures at the feet of President Johnson. In 1909, W.E.B. Du Bois gave a presentation to the American Historical Association in New York in which he directly challenged the Dunning theory.

Du Bois claimed Reconstruction had important successes, including free public schools for the South and progressive social programs.

After a 1908 race riot in Springfield, Illinois, Black and white activists formed a new civil rights group called the National Association for the Advancement of Colored People (NAACP)—which is still active today. The group's mission was to end racial prejudice and work to ensure the political, social, and economic equality of African Americans. The group was put to the test a few years later when the film, *The Birth of a Nation*, was released in theaters in 1915.

The Birth of a Nation cemented the national view that Reconstruction had been a total failure. The movie was directed by D.W. Griffith (1875–1948), the son of a Confederate cavalry officer, based on a play written by Thomas Dixon Jr. (1864–1946). The plot of the three-hour movie centered on a Black man who raped a teenage white girl and was captured and killed by the Klan. The Black characters were played by whites with their faces painted Black. In a historical first, the film was previewed for President Woodrow Wilson (1856–1924) at the White House. A journalist quoted him as saying he enjoyed it.

RECONSTRUCT

Most white historians, however, ignored the scholarship of Lynch, Du Bois, and others and remained devoted to the Dunning theory for the next half century.

THE NIAGARA MOVEMENT

On July 11, 1905, 29 Black men met in Niagara Falls, Canada, to form a new civil rights group. The writers, businessmen, teachers, and clergy had tried to meet in New York, but no hotel would admit them. The Niagara Movement did not ask for rights, it demanded them. The group's manifesto said, "We claim for ourselves every single right that belongs to a freeborn American . . . and until we get these rights we will never cease to protest and assail the ears of America." The Niagara Movement disbanded after only a few years because it lacked funding.

African Americans were alarmed by the passion aroused in white audiences as they watched the film. In Houston, viewers screamed, "Lynch him!" while watching the Black villain chase a white girl. In Lafayette, Indiana, a man shot and killed a teenage Black boy after watching the movie.

The NAACP called for the film to be boycotted.

The governor of Ohio, a Republican and son of a Union soldier, banned the film in his state because it was "mob-inciting." Most theaters in Massachusetts stopped showing the film because so many fights broke out between Blacks and whites outside theaters. The movie was still shown in the rest of the country, however, and white audiences flocked to see it.

Next, the NAACP tried to have the film censored. At that time, the National Board of Censorship gave movies a seal of approval if they met decency standards. The board had already approved *The Birth of a Nation*. The recommendation to censor the film was controversial because the First Amendment to the Constitution protects freedom of speech and expression.

The board of censorship contacted the White House. When the board members learned that President Wilson had seen the movie and liked it, the board refused to withdraw their approval of the film.

Then, Edward White (1845–1921), chief justice of the U.S. Supreme Court, publicly endorsed the movie. White had been a Confederate soldier and a member of the Klan. By the end of 1917, *The Birth of a Nation* had grossed $60 million, an astounding sum of money for the time.

RECONSTRUCT

Riling up the public had been the intention of Thomas Dixon Jr., the author of the novel on which *The Birth of a Nation* was based. During an interview, Dixon said the main purpose of the book "was to create a feeling of abhorrence in white people, against colored men . . ." and he "wished to have all Negroes removed from the United States."

"The white men were roused by a mere instinct of self-preservation . . . until at last there had sprung into existence a great Ku Klux Klan, a veritable empire of the South, to protect the Southern country."

—Woodrow Wilson's quote from the movie, *The Birth of a Nation*

Boycotting and censoring did not work, so Black writers, journalists, filmmakers, and academics made their own creative work about the true history of Reconstruction.

In 1920, filmmaker Oscar Micheaux (1884–1951) produced *Within Our Gates*, a film that turned *The Birth of a Nation* on its head. The story was about a Black teacher whose parents were lynched and who narrowly missed being raped by a white man. Few white people, however, saw the movie.

NOT MERELY A COMMON MOVING PICTURE A SCREEN MASTERPIECE — "Within Our Gates" — THE PLAY OF THE HOUR ALL RECORDS BROKEN DONT MISS IT — ONE DAY ONLY — FEATURING, EVELYN PREER — SPECIAL MUSIC — SUPPORTED BY AN ALL STAR COLORED CAST — UNION HALL, KENT & AURORA AVES. — "THE LYNCHING EVIL" — MANAGEMENT, J. HOMER GOINS — WHO KILLED PHILIP GIRDLESTONE? — 8000 FEET OF SENSATIONAL REALISM 8000 — Oscar Micheaux's Within Our Gates A Story of the Negro — Monday Evening — July 12, 8:30 p.m. — SPECIAL NOTICE! Owing to the peculiar nature of this picture no theatre could be secured that would exhibit it, therefore we were forced to do the next best thing and use our own building. — ADMISSION 50 CENTS

African American writers pushed back, too. In 1935, W.E.B. Du Bois published *Black Reconstruction in America*. At more than 700 pages, this book tried to set the record straight. In a chapter titled "The Propaganda of History," Du Bois challenged whites who ignored evidence that did not support their theories about Black inferiority. He described the Dunning School as "propaganda against the Negro." These authors, Du Bois argued, did not give voice to "the chief witness in Reconstruction, the emancipated slave himself."

Du Bois's analysis did not reshape public opinion because few whites read his book. The editors of the academic journal that reviewed history books ignored Du Bois's work. *Time* magazine labeled him "an ax grinder."

In its first year, *Black Reconstruction in America* sold only 376 copies.

SLAVE REPARATIONS

On June 19, 2019, activists and lawmakers gathered in the U.S. Capitol for a hearing on whether the federal government should make reparations to the descendants of enslaved people. Republican Senate Majority Leader Mitch McConnell (1942–) does not think modern Americans should have to pay damages "for something that happened 150 years ago, for whom none of us currently living are responsible." Today, the worth of the government's broken promise to give 4 million emancipated slaves 40 acres each is between $1.5 and $2 trillion. In addition, an estimated 11 million acres of land owned by Blacks after Reconstruction ended were taken through violence, fraud, and theft, some of it as recently as the 1980s. Writer Ta-Nehisi Coates (1975–) believes the descendants of slaves deserve reparations because they were exploited long after slavery was abolished. Coates said, "It was 150 years ago, and it was right now."

African Americans, on the other hand, welcomed the book. Black journalists reviewed it. Black teachers and ministers discussed the book with their communities. Black readers who could not afford their own copies formed book lovers clubs in which they bought one copy and passed it from member to member.

When the Civil Rights Movement began in the mid-1950s, American attitudes about race slowly began to shift again.

By the 1960s, mainstream historians and scholars were reexamining what early-twentieth-century Black writers had to say about Reconstruction. Some scholars began to revise the history of Reconstruction once again. Only this time, their conclusions were based on evidence rather than myths of white supremacy.

FAILURE OR SUCCESS?

W.E.B. Du Bois wrote, "The slave went free; stood a brief moment in the sun; then moved back again toward slavery." The term "back toward slavery" implies that Reconstruction was a failure. Yet, Du Bois also mentions that "brief moment in the sun." Depending on the evidence, Reconstruction was both a failure and a success.

One of the major weaknesses of Reconstruction was the lack of land reform. When the Johnson administration went back on the government's promise to give freedmen 40 acres, most Southern Blacks became sharecroppers. As a result, during the last 150 years, a wealth gap between Blacks and whites has become a chasm.

Reconstruction also failed because it could not shake the South's firm belief in white supremacy. This ideology led to a half a century of Jim Crow. It took the Civil Rights Movement to dismantle the system of legal segregation that spread throughout the South after Reconstruction ended.

White supremacy, however, is still rooted in American culture and institutions. According to a 2018 Pacific Research Institute poll, one-third of white Americans believe the expectation that non-white people will make up the majority of the U.S. population by 2045 is "mostly negative."

Another criticism modern historians make about Reconstruction is that the federal government did not do enough to stop domestic terrorism. The brutality of the Klan, the White League, the Red Shirts, and other violent groups is what ultimately doomed Black participation in government.

Domestic terrorism still exists and is on the upswing. Additionally, according to the Southern Poverty Law Center, the number of hate groups in the United States reached a record high of 1,020 organizations in 2018.

In 2019, African Americans made up 13 percent of the population, but owned less than 3 percent of the nation's wealth.

RECONSTRUCT

Many white supremacist groups stoke fears of white genocide. Their leaders insist that unless something drastic is done, America's white population will disappear.

Despite these serious flaws, **Reconstruction was truly a revolutionary time in the United States.**

It was a period of biracial democracy in the South. Lawmakers crafted progressive state constitutions. Forward-thinking governments created the South's first public education system and first mental health hospitals.

Even when Reconstruction ended and Southern Blacks lost their political and civil rights, their world was better in fundamental ways. The independent Black family remained intact. The seeds of educational progress had been planted and would grow. Intellectuals would emerge from the Black universities founded during Reconstruction to lead the Civil Rights Movement in the mid-twentieth century. During Reconstruction, Black people formed religious, economic, social, and political networks that survived and laid the foundation for the Black middle class.

Five female officers of the Women's League, Newport, Rhode Island, 1899

While the Reconstruction era amendments were not enforced when Reconstruction ended, they did not disappear. Black people remained citizens. They could move freely, and millions did. When the United States entered World War I in 1914, manufacturing jobs opened up in Northern states, and Southern Blacks moved North during what was called the "Great Migration."

Black activists and their allies always saw the potential for the Fourteenth and Fifteenth Amendments.

During the Civil Rights Movement, lawyers based their challenges to discriminatory laws on the rights contained in these amendments. Slowly, and with great sacrifice, Southern Blacks regained the political and civil rights that had been the heart of Reconstruction reforms.

Reconstruction did not fail. But a sustained campaign of intimidation and violence that was supported by a belief in white supremacy ground down the Reconstruction revolution. It is this belief in white supremacy that remains the challenging legacy of Reconstruction.

LESSONS FOR THE PRESENT

History is not a straightforward march of progress. The Reconstruction era proves that rights and liberties once gained can be lost.

This can be seen today in the right to vote. By 1900, Southern states had erected obstacles, such as literacy tests and poll taxes, to prevent Blacks from voting. Finally, in 1965, Congress passed the Voting Rights Act and Southern Blacks could once again freely go to the polls. However, in 2013, the U.S. Supreme Court invalidated a key portion of this law, and activists are worried that this will cause hardships at the polls.

Reconstruction also revealed that, although a law can abolish slavery, it cannot erase the racism that allowed slavery to exist in the first place. The violence in Charlottesville in 2017 is evidence of this. People are willing to commit acts of terror to protect Confederate monuments from being dismantled.

Reconstruction was a revolution—and it remains unfinished. The United States is still under reconstruction. Slavery was abolished, but Americans have yet to figure out how to create a multiracial society with equality and justice for all. That work is left for twenty-first century Americans to complete.

KEY QUESTIONS

• **Will Reconstruction ever be complete? How will Americans know?**

Since the 2010 election, many states have put tougher voting rules into place. Those who support these measures claim they reduce voter fraud. Those who oppose them say these rules discourage people from voting. How could you find out whose argument is the most accurate?

Go to the map at this website to see if the state where you live has passed voting restrictions.

Brennan Center
voting restrictions

TEXT TO WORLD

What role will you choose to play in the spread of racial equality? How?

AN UNFINISHED REVOLUTION

In what ways has America made progress toward the ideals of freedom and equality since the Reconstruction era? In what areas does society fall short of those ideals?

VOCAB LAB

Write down what you think each word means. What root words can you find to help you? What does the context of the word tell you?

boycott, **censor**, **Lost Cause**, **propaganda**, **reparations**, **sanitize**, and **segregation**.

Compare your definitions with those of your friends or classmates. Did you all come up with the same meanings? Turn to the text and glossary if you need help.

- **Head to the library or use the internet to research the state of equality in areas important to freedpeople during Reconstruction.** Consider the following:

  - political participation

  - access to education

  - economic prosperity

  - social equality.

- **Record your findings.** In what areas has America become more equal and in what areas is there evidence of inequality? How did you measure progress or lack of it?

- **Choose a medium to display your findings.** Suggestions include an essay, poster, painting, collage, or poem. How can you make your research interesting and engaging?

> To investigate more, reflect on how you can use your voice and actions to make a positive difference in the world. What issues need to be championed in your community? How can you help to create positive change?

GLOSSARY

abhorrence: extreme hatred.

abolish: to completely do away with something.

abolitionist: a person who supported ending slavery.

acquit: to find someone not guilty of a crime.

activist: a person who works to bring about social or political change.

adjourn: to temporarily suspend a meeting until a future time.

ally: a partner in support of a cause.

amendment: a change made to a law or document.

amnesty: a government pardon for a person who has committed a crime.

aristocracy: a class of people who hold high rank and privilege.

arsonist: someone who deliberately sets a fire to destroy property.

article: a document.

assassination: murder committed for political rather than personal reasons.

bankrupt: to be unable to repay debts.

barrage: to bombard someone.

bias: the tendency to see or think of things a certain way based on previously held prejudices or beliefs.

biracial: involving members of two races.

birthright citizenship: citizenship automatically granted to a child born in a particular country, regardless of whether the child's parents are citizens.

Black Codes: a series of laws imposed in the South after the Civil War that tried to force Blacks back into plantation work.

boycott: to refuse to use, buy, or deal with a business as a protest of that company's policies.

bribery: money or other favors given to influence a person in a position of authority or power.

brokerage house: a company that provides financial services.

cabinet: senior advisers to the president who administer the policies of federal departments.

capacity: the ability to do something.

carpetbagger: a negative term used to label Northerners who moved to the South after the Civil War.

censor: to examine a book or movie before publication and remove unacceptable parts.

citizen: a person who has all the rights and responsibilities that come with being a full member of a country.

citizenship: legally belonging to a country and having the rights and protection of that country.

civil rights: rights of citizens to have political and social freedom and equality.

Civil Rights Movement: a struggle during the 1950s and 1960s in the United States for Blacks to gain equal rights under the law.

Civil War: the war in the United States, from 1861 to 1865, between the states in the North and the slave-owning states in the South. A civil war is a war between citizens of the same country.

commemoration: serving as a memorial.

commoner: an ordinary person without rank or title.

compensate: to give something, usually money, in recognition of loss, suffering, or injury incurred.

compulsory: something that must be done.

concession: to yield or give up a right, privilege, or point in an argument.

condemn: to express disapproval of or sentence someone to punishment.

Confederate: the government established by the Southern slave-owning states of the United States after they left the Union in 1860 and 1861. Called the Confederate States of America or the Confederacy. Also someone who worked for or believed in the cause of the Confederate States of America.

confiscate: to take property.

conservative: someone who prefers traditional customs and laws rather than major change.

conspire: to secretly plan to do something wrong or harmful.

GLOSSARY

constitution: the basic principles and laws of a nation or state.

constitutional convention: a meeting during which a constitution is created or changed.

controversial: an issue that causes disagreement.

convention: a formal meeting to discuss a certain issue.

convict: to declare someone guilty of a criminal offense.

corruption: the dishonest or illegal behavior of people in power.

counter-protest: a protest staged to counter or oppose another protest.

countermand: to recall an order.

counterrevolution: a movement to overthrow a government formed by a previous revolution.

culture: the beliefs and way of life of a group of people, which can include religion, language, art, clothing, food, and holidays.

death knell: an indication that something will soon be destroyed or dead.

debt: a service or money owed.

deed: a legal document that proves someone is the owner of something.

delegate: a person chosen to represent other people at a convention.

deprive: to deny someone the use or possession of something.

discrimination: the unjust treatment of some groups of people based on their race, religion, or gender.

disenfranchise: to take away the right to vote.

disillusioned: feeling disappointment from finding out that something isn't as good as it was thought to be.

dismantle: to take apart.

distortion: changing something out of its true, natural, or original state.

district attorney: an elected or appointed official who represents the government when prosecuting a crime.

domestic terrorism: political violence in which victims and perpetrators are citizens of the same country.

Dunning School: the early-twentieth-century historical theory that argued Reconstruction was flawed and was a time when the federal government abused its power.

economic: having to do with the resources and wealth of a country.

economic depression: a lasting, long-term downturn in a country's economic activity.

Electoral College: a group of electors chosen by the people in each state to formally vote for the president and vice president of the United States.

emancipate: to legally free someone.

Emancipation Proclamation: the announcement made by President Lincoln during the Civil War on September 22, 1862, emancipating all slaves in the Confederacy. It went into effect on January 1, 1863.

embed: to install something permanently inside something else.

emblem: a design or image that represents something.

embolden: to give someone the courage or confidence to do something.

endorse: to declare public approval or support of.

enfranchise: to grant the right to vote.

enslave: to make someone a slave.

equality: being treated the same, with the same rights and opportunities as others.

era: a period of time marked by a particular set of events.

evict: to force someone from a property.

exalt: to raise in rank or honor.

executive branch: the branch of the U.S. government that carries out laws and includes the president, vice president, cabinet members, and others.

exile: banishment from living in a certain place.

federal: related to the central government of a country.

feminist: a person who believes men and women should have equal rights and opportunities.

GLOSSARY

Fifteenth Amendment: an amendment to the U.S. Constitution, ratified in 1870, that guaranteed Black men the right to vote.

foreclose: to take possession of someone's property when they cannot pay the debt on it.

Fourteenth Amendment: an amendment to the U.S. Constitution, ratified in 1868, that grants citizenship to all persons born or naturalized in the United States, including former enslaved people, and guarantees all citizens equal protection of the laws.

freedom: the ability to choose and act without constraints.

freedpeople: people who were freed from slavery.

gallery: a balcony on the upper floor of a hall or chamber where the audience sits.

genocide: the deliberate killing of a large group of people based on race, ethnicity, or nationality.

Great Migration: the movement of millions of African Americans from the South to the North, Midwest, and West between 1916 and 1970.

harmonious: free from disagreement or dissent.

heritage: the cultural traditions and history of a group of people.

high crimes and misdemeanors: a phrase from the U.S. Constitution that spells out what a president can be impeached for.

homestead: a dwelling and the land that goes with it.

icon: a widely recognized symbol of a certain time or a person or thing that grows to represent a larger idea.

idealist: a person who tries to follow noble principles and goals.

illiterate: not being able to read or write.

impartial: fair, without bias or prejudice.

impeach: to formally charge a public official with a crime or misconduct.

implement: a tool or other piece of equipment or to put a plan to work.

incentive: a reward that encourages someone to do something.

inference: a conclusion reached by evidence and reasoning.

inflame: to arouse violent feelings.

infographic: a visual representation of data, information, or knowledge.

injunction: an order from a court that tells someone to do or not do a certain act.

integrate: to bring people of different races together.

interracial: existing between or involving different races of people.

intimidation: the act of making another person fearful with threats or other shows of power.

invalidate: to make something not legal or official.

ironic: an event or situation that is interesting and sometimes humorous because it is the opposite of what you would expect.

irrespective: not taking something into account.

Jim Crow: a collection of state and local laws that legalized racial segregation in the South.

jurisdiction: the authority to interpret and apply the law.

juror: someone who is part of a jury, which is a group of citizens who hear a case in court and give their opinion, called a verdict.

justice: fair action or treatment based on the law.

Ku Klux Klan (KKK): a terrorist group formed after the Civil War that believes white Christians should hold the power in society.

lament: a passionate expression of grief or sorrow.

land redistribution: to take land from one group of individuals and give it to another.

legacy: something handed down from the past that has a long-lasting impact.

legislative branch: the branch of the U.S. government that makes the laws. It includes the U.S. Senate and the U.S. House of Representatives.

legislator: someone who works to make laws.

lenient: not severe or strong enough punishment for wrongdoing.

liberty: freedom, the ability to act or live as one chooses.

GLOSSARY

literate: having the ability to read.

Lost Cause: an interpretation of the Civil War that presents the war from the point of view of the Confederates and ignores historical evidence.

lynch: to illegally execute a person, usually by hanging.

manifesto: a public statement of your views or intentions to do something.

massacre: the deliberate killing of many people.

midterm elections: an election held two years into a presidential term.

migrant: a person who moves from place to place to find work.

misdemeanor: a criminal offense that is less serious than a felony.

missionary: a person sent on a religious mission.

moderate: someone who believes political and social change should be slow and steady.

monument: a building, structure, or statue that is special because it honors an event or person, or because it is beautiful.

Moses: a holy man in the Christian bible who led the Hebrew people out of slavery.

NAACP: National Association for the Advancement of Colored People, a group formed in the early twentieth century to advance justice for African Americans.

naturalize: to make someone a citizen.

neutralize: to stop something from having an effect.

notorious: famous or well known, usually for a bad deed.

offensive: describes something that causes someone to feel deeply hurt, upset, or angry.

override: to disregard or set aside.

paramilitary: an unofficial military force.

pardon: to officially excuse someone for something they have done.

perpetrator: a person who does a harmful, illegal, or immoral act.

petition: to formally request something from the government.

pivotal: vitally important.

political: relating to the government or the public affairs of a certain place.

poll tax: a payment to the government that was sometimes required before a person was allowed the right to vote.

prejudice: an unfair feeling of dislike for a person or group, usually based on gender, race, or religion.

prejudicial: harmful to someone or something.

presidential pardon: when the president officially grants forgiveness to someone for something they have done.

progressive: in favor of progress, change, improvement, or reform.

prohibit: to make illegal.

propaganda: biased, misleading, or false information that is promoted to persuade people to believe a certain viewpoint.

prosecutor: a lawyer who represents the state or the people in a criminal trial.

race relations: relations between members or communities of different races within one country.

racial equality: treating everyone the same, regardless of race or skin color.

racism: negative opinions or treatment of people based on race and the notion that people of a different race are inferior because of their race.

racist: describes the hatred of people of a different race.

radical: favoring drastic political, economic, or social reforms.

Radical Republicans: a group of politicians within the Republican Party from around 1854 until the end of Reconstruction in 1877 who had the goal of immediate, complete, permanent eradication of slavery.

ratification: to formally approve a law or treaty.

rations: the food allowance for one day.

rebel: a person who resists the rules or government of the society he or she lives in. Also to fight against authority or someone fighting against authority.

recede: to become more distant or move away.

reconcile: to cause people or groups to become friendly again after an argument.

Reconstruction: the period of time after the Civil War in which the states that had seceded were brought back into the United States.

reconvene: to come together again for a public purpose.

redeemer: someone who brings goodness or honor to something again.

redemption: being saved from sin, error, or evil.

redistribute: to pass out something in a different way.

reform: a change to improve something.

reparation: the act of making amends for a past injury.

repeal: to cancel a law.

reprehensible: deserving of blame.

representation: a person or group that speaks or acts for or in support of another person or group.

romanticize: to idealize something or someone.

sanction: to approve. Also a penalty for disobeying a law or rule.

sanitize: to make something better by removing unpleasant features.

scalawag: a term for a white Southerner who supported Reconstruction polices after the Civil War.

secede: to formally withdraw from a political union.

segregation: the enforced separation of different racial groups in a community or country.

session: the gathering together of legislators to conduct official business.

sharecropper: a farmer in the Southern United States during Reconstruction who was provided with land, tools, seed, and living quarters in return for a portion of the harvested crop.

slavery: the use of enslaved people as workers. An enslaved person is owned by another person and forced to work, without pay, against their will.

social: relating to activities that involve being with other people and rules about behavior with other people.

social justice: when people are treated fairly and equally within a society.

storyboard: a series of graphic drawings or images that are arranged consecutively to show changes in action or scene.

stupor: a state of near-unconsciousness.

suffrage: the right to vote.

suffragette: female activists who wanted women to have voting rights.

supremacist: a person who holds the racist belief that white people are superior to those of all other races.

suspend: to stop something temporarily or to officially stop someone from doing their job or from going to school for a limited time.

terrorism: the unlawful use of violence and intimidation, especially against civilians, in the pursuit of political aims.

Thirteenth Amendment: an amendment to the U.S. Constitution, ratified in 1865, that abolished slavery and involuntary servitude except as punishment for a crime.

thrifty: to not waste money or resources.

title: the legal ownership of a piece of property.

treason: the crime of betraying one's country.

tyrant: a cruel ruler who denies people their rights.

unconstitutional: an act or policy that violates the U.S. Constitution and is, therefore, illegal.

Union: the term used for the federal (national) government of the United States in the Civil War, which also referred to the Northern states.

vagrant: a homeless, jobless person.

values: strongly held beliefs about what is valuable, important, or acceptable.

veto: the power given to the executive branch to cancel or postpone the decisions of the legislative branch.

vocation: a preference or calling to a specific job.

white supremacy: the belief that white people are naturally superior to all other races and that whites should have control over people of other races.

RESOURCES

BOOKS

Bolden, Tonya. *Cause: Reconstruction America, 1863-1877*. Alfred Knopf, 2005.

Bolden, Tonya, and Gates Jr., Henry Louis. *Dark Sky Rising: Reconstruction and the Dawn of Jim Crow*. Scholastic, 2019.

Gordon-Reed, Annette. *Andrew Johnson*. Henry Holt & Co., 2011.

VIDEOS

Reconstruction. Marchesi, Julia, director. PBS, 2019.

MUSEUMS

National Museum of African American History & Culture
nmaahc.si.edu

The Old Slave Mart Museum in Charleston, South Carolina
charleston-sc.gov/160/Old-Slave-Mart-Museum

Reconstruction Era National Historic Park
nps.gov/reer/index.htm

WEBSITES

Digital History
digitalhistory.uh.edu

The Civil War and Reconstruction: 1861-1877
loc.gov/teachers/classroommaterials/presentationsandactivities/presentations/timeline/civilwar

Freedmen and Southern Society Project, University of Maryland
freedmen.umd.edu/index.html

SELECTED BIBLIOGRAPHY

Egerton, Douglas R. *The Wars of Reconstruction: The Brief, Violent History of America's Most Progressive Era*. Bloomsbury Press, 2014.

Foner, Eric. *A Short History of Reconstruction*. Harper Perennial, 2014.

Gates Jr., Henry Louis. *Stony the Road: Reconstruction, White Supremacy, and the Rise of Jim Crow*. Penguin, 2019.

Langguth. A.J. *After Lincoln: How the North Won the Civil War and Lost the Peace*. Simon & Schuster, 2014

Rose, Willie Lee. *Rehearsal for Reconstruction: The Port Royal Experiment*. Bobbs-Merrill Co., 1964.

Sterling, Dorothy (ed.). *We Are Your Sisters: Black Women in the Nineteenth Century*. W.W. Norton, 1984.

RESOURCES

QR CODE GLOSSARY

Page 4: google.com/maps/d/u/0/viewer?mid=15O4IHHI41rWplhax6z_ak238m h4eFqpQ&ll=38.19943672148611%2C-96.88488949999999&z=4

Page 17: digitalhistory.uh.edu/disp_textbook.cfm?smtID=3&psid=518

Page 21: youtube.com/watch?v=FwREAW4SlVY

Page 24: hnoc.org/database/lost-friends/index.html

Page 24: informationwanted.org

Page 29: loc.gov/resource/ds.07129

Page 30: teachingamericanhistory.org/library/document/black-codes-of-mississippi

Page 41: loc.gov/resource/cph.3a41094

Page 44: teachingamericanhistory.org/library/document/reply-of-the-colored-delegation-to-the-president

Page 47: house.gov

Page 47: senate.gov

Page 47: nces.ed.gov/nceskids/createagraph

Page 52: docsteach.org/documents/document/petition-prohibit-disfranchisement

Page 55: etc.usf.edu/maps/pages/2800/2853/2853.htm

Page 66: nytimes.com/video/us/politics/100000006788245/impeachment-process-history.html?action=click&gtype=vhs&version=vhs-heading&module=vhs&region=title-area&cview=true&t=5

Page 78: facinghistory.org/reconstruction-era/black-officeholders-south

Page 84: digital.archives.alabama.gov/cdm/singleitem/collection/voices/id/1746

Page 89: explorehistory.ou.edu/wp-content/uploads/2013/07/Post-war-Paper-1-SOURCE-DOC-3-ACv1.pdf

Page 96: lynchinginamerica.eji.org

Page 96: statesanctioned.com/teaching-about-lynching

Page 100: babel.hathitrust.org/cgi/pt?id=loc.ark:/13960/t9n304c2r&view=1up&seq=424

Page 107: brennancenter.org/our-work/research-reports/new-voting-restrictions-america

INDEX

INDEX